365 Pocket® Prayers for Women

Guidance and Wisdom for Each New Day

Tyndale House Publishers, Carol Stream, Illinois

Visit Tyndale online at tyndale.com.

365 Pocket Prayers for Women: Guidance and Wisdom for Each New Day

Designed by Alberto C. Navata Jr.

Edited by Amy Mason

For information about special discounts for bulk purchases, please contact Tyndale House Publishers at csresponse@tyndale.com, or call 1-855-277-9400.

ISBN 978-1-4143-6290-8 (LeatherLike)
ISBN 978-1-4964-1171-6 (sc)

Printed in the United States of America

27 26 25 24 23 22 21
12 11 10 9 8 7 6

INTRODUCTION

Prayer is simply talking with God. As women of faith, we can come to him anytime, approach him anywhere, and pray about anything. God loves our honest, heartfelt prayers, and he cares deeply for the details of our lives. As we come before him with praise or petition, we demonstrate that we trust him and long to draw near to him.

Perhaps your faith is relatively new and you're not yet comfortable praying. This book is for you. The prayers we've developed can be claimed as your own conversations with God. As you pray through each topic and day, we hope you will become more comfortable talking with God and will even begin to form your own prayers to him.

Perhaps you've been a believer for years but need a little inspiration in your prayer life. This book is for you, too. We all have times when we repeat the same prayers over and over. By including a year's worth of unique prayers that cover a broad range of topics, this book will help rejuvenate your dialogue with God.

Thank God that we don't have to be spiritually mature or "on fire" to have a meaningful prayer life! Wherever you are in your spiritual journey, God is delighted when you draw near to him. We hope this little book will help you do so.

You will find 365 prayers, arranged by days and topics. You can pray through each day of the year consecutively if you wish. Alternatively, look in the index for a topic that will help you pray through an urgent need or give words to something you may be experiencing. Every few days you will also find prayers called *Prayerful Moments.* These are shorter prayers for days when time is limited or for when you need a quick word with God.

As you enter into a new prayer, take it slow. Spend some time thinking about what you're saying to God, and try to personalize each prayer for your own life. Making each written prayer your own honest praise or petition will make it more meaningful.

In your conversations with God, take some time to listen. Reading God's Word as a part of your prayer time gives the Lord an opportunity to speak to you, too. You won't want to miss what he has to say! We've included a Scripture verse at the end of each prayer to help you ponder what God might be communicating to you.

Thank you for joining us on this quest for a deeper prayer life. It is our hope that by the end of this book, you will be inspired in your conversations with God and—most important—feel closer to him than ever before. It is often in these special times of prayer that God does his powerful work in our hearts. So don't give up; stick with it. As his Word says to us, "Let us come boldly to the throne of our gracious God. There we will receive his mercy, and we will find grace to help us when we need it most" (Hebrews 4:16).

The privilege of prayer is that it ushers us straight into the presence of our loving God. And Scripture promises us that he won't disappoint! With that in mind, it's time to begin.

A prayer about BLESSINGS
When I want to experience God's blessings

MERCIFUL GOD,
Your love is like an ocean, and wave after wave of your blessings flow over me. Your Word says that you have promised rich blessings to those who love you, including your presence, your grace, your comfort, your provision, and your eternal peace. What abundant riches! I am overwhelmed by your love and generosity toward me; my cup overflows. O Lord, may I always respond to your blessings with gratitude and obedience. And guard me from desiring blessing just for my own benefit so that I can live a comfortable life. I know that would be misunderstanding your purpose, which is to bless me so that I can bless others. May your love and grace flow through me.

You prepare a feast for me in the presence of my enemies. You honor me by anointing my head with oil. My cup overflows with blessings. Surely your goodness and unfailing love will pursue me all the days of my life, and I will live in the house of the LORD forever. PSALM 23:5-6

A prayer about GOALS
When I want to set goals for my life

HEAVENLY FATHER,
I don't want to meander through life doing whatever seems right at the moment. I want my life to count for something! I know that if I don't set goals, I won't achieve much of consequence. Please give me the discipline to set wise goals, both short term and long term, but help me never to forget that the most important goals of all are eternal. Material success and fame are only temporal, but my relationship with you and the results of service to you will last forever. May I plan for eternity, thinking carefully about what will endure. Teach me to filter my earthly goals through the lens of eternity; then I will know the goals that matter. How can I please you? How can I draw close to you? When you are my focus, my earthly priorities will fall into place.

We are always confident, even though we know that as long as we live in these bodies we are not at home with the Lord. For we live by believing and not by seeing. . . . So whether we are here in this body or away from this body, our goal is to please him. 2 CORINTHIANS 5:6-7, 9

A prayer about CHALLENGES

When I need to accept the difficulties that come into my life

DEAR GOD,

I know that I live in a fallen world. Jesus himself told his disciples that in this world they would have trouble—and I'm having trouble right now. Lord, I don't like what is happening in my life. I'm struggling, but I know that it's possible for me to accept my circumstances without liking them. Please help me to remember that I have a glorious future in heaven. As I keep eternity in mind, may I grow through the difficulties I experience now and may I remember that those difficulties will end with this earthly life. Train me to accept what comes from your hand and to trust that you have something to teach me through whatever comes my way.

What we suffer now is nothing compared to the glory he will reveal to us later. . . . We believers . . . groan, even though we have the Holy Spirit within us as a foretaste of future glory, for we long for our bodies to be released from sin and suffering. We . . . wait with eager hope for the day when God will give us our full rights as his adopted children, including the new bodies he has promised us.

ROMANS 8:18, 23

DAY 4

A prayer about HEALING

When I wonder whether God can heal my hurts

O GREAT PHYSICIAN,

You made my body, and you can certainly repair and restore it. You made my mind and soul, and you can repair and restore those, too. You are the great healer, not bound by the limitations of this world. I believe you can intervene to overcome any threat to my life, including illness or disease—physical, mental, spiritual, or emotional. O Lord, I have faith that you are able to intervene, but sometimes I doubt that you will. Yet I know from your Word that you love me enough to have died for me, and you promise that in eternity I will be fully healed. Thank you. Those two assurances give me what I need to endure and to wait for your healing power to make me whole—whether in this life or in eternity. May I be patient and trust you to do what is best in my life.

For you who fear my name, the Sun of Righteousness will rise with healing in his wings. And you will go free, leaping with joy like calves let out to pasture. MALACHI 4:2

DAY 5

A prayer about NEEDS
When I'm trying to be content

LOVING FATHER,
I'm struggling with lack of contentment, and I know the problem is that I'm getting my wants mixed up with my needs. To survive, I need basic things such as food, water, shelter, and love—when I have those things, I should be content. But too often I'm consumed with my wants. Even when they're fulfilled, they leave me unsatisfied, discontented, and looking for more. And when I want things that oppose your desires, I find myself increasingly consumed with jealousy, covetousness, deceit, or materialism. Help me, Lord! Teach me the difference between my needs and my wants so that I may find contentment in living your way. As you meet my needs, show me your power and provision, and let me learn that you are sufficient. Refocus my mind on your values instead of on my own. Then I will no longer be grasping for something else; instead, I will have a heart full of gratitude for what you have already provided.

Don't love money; be satisfied with what you have. For God has said, "I will never fail you. I will never abandon you."
HEBREWS 13:5

DAY 6 *Prayerful Moment*

A prayer about HELPLESSNESS
When there's nothing I can do

FATHER,

I cry out to you today in desperate need. I am struggling, downcast, and completely helpless—I need you! When I try to get myself out of trouble, I miss out on seeing what you can do in my life. You are the one who loves doing the impossible, so I reach out to you, my lifeline, and trust that you will help me.

Asa cried out to the LORD his God, "O LORD, no one but you can help the powerless against the mighty! Help us, O LORD our God, for we trust in you alone."

2 CHRONICLES 14:11

DAY 7 *Prayerful Moment*

A prayer about FRIENDSHIP
When I want God to strengthen my friendships

LORD,

Thank you for the friends you have given me. We are glued together with bonds of loyalty and commitment, no matter what the external circumstances are. May I be a good friend to them and love them with genuine Christian love. Work in my heart so that I may be loyal, helpful, patient, kind, and forgiving.

Love is patient and kind. Love is not jealous or boastful or proud or rude. It does not demand its own way.

1 CORINTHIANS 13:4-5

A prayer about CHILDREN

When I consider what children can teach me about trusting God

HEAVENLY FATHER,

In children I see the innocence, curiosity, and faith that are so dear to you. Children are eager to experience new adventures and learn about the world around them, and they trust their parents to guide them, comfort them, and meet their needs. Father, I know you want me to approach life the same way. May I be willing to follow you on the adventure of life, learn all I can about you, and trust you for all I need. I sometimes make life too complicated, but you invite me simply to trust you. And may my faith be straightforward and honest as I anticipate with delight the blessings of divine moments with you. You are my Father, and I am your child.

[Jesus] said, "I tell you the truth, unless you turn from your sins and become like little children, you will never get into the Kingdom of Heaven. So anyone who becomes as humble as this little child is the greatest in the Kingdom of Heaven." MATTHEW 18:3-4

DAY 9

A prayer about RENEWAL
When I need a fresh start

LORD,

Your Word makes clear that you will restore any heart that seeks a new start. That's what I want! My desire is to turn to you and away from the sin that has been bringing me down, so please forgive my sin, Lord. I know that left unconfessed, it would poison everything I do. I'm thankful that your forgiveness is not dependent on the magnitude of my sin but on the magnitude of your love. The only sin that is too great for your unconditional love and forgiveness is an attitude of hostile rejection that would prevent someone from accepting your forgiveness. You won't force your love on anyone, but your compassion is available to all who seek it. May I never reject your love, Lord. Please soften my heart—mold it and prepare me for the renewal that only your Spirit can bring.

Throw off your old sinful nature and your former way of life, which is corrupted by lust and deception. Instead, let the Spirit renew your thoughts and attitudes. Put on your new nature, created to be like God—truly righteous and holy.

EPHESIANS 4:22-24

DAY 10

A prayer about HEAVEN

When I look forward to being with God forever

LORD,

You have planted within me a desire for more than just this life. I was created for something that is missing from this world, and I yearn for it. You made me in your image, with eternal value, so nothing but you, the eternal God, can truly satisfy this longing. Thank you for giving me glimpses—through nature, art, and relationships—of the perfect world that will be found only in heaven. I look forward with gladness to the day when you will restore the earth to the way it was when you first created it. I praise you because eternity will be a never-ending exploration of heaven's beauty and your character, and I will never tire of what you have prepared for me.

[Jesus said,] "Don't let your hearts be troubled. Trust in God, and trust also in me. There is more than enough room in my Father's home. If this were not so, would I have told you that I am going to prepare a place for you? When everything is ready, I will come and get you, so that you will always be with me where I am." JOHN 14:1-3

A prayer about CONFESSION
When my sin separates me from God

HEAVENLY FATHER,

Today I'm feeling guilty about something I've done. I know you don't intend for me to live with this guilt, but it has a purpose: it prompts me to confess my wrong to you. Lord, you know that I want things to be right between us. I admit my wrong and receive your cleansing forgiveness. Because I have confessed my sin and turned away from it, you have promised to remove my guilt, restore my joy, and heal my broken soul with your forgiving love.

Oh, what joy for those whose disobedience is forgiven, whose sin is put out of sight! Yes, what joy for those whose record the LORD has cleared of guilt, whose lives are lived in complete honesty! When I refused to confess my sin, my body wasted away, and I groaned all day long. . . . Finally, I confessed all my sins to you and stopped trying to hide my guilt. I said to myself, "I will confess my rebellion to the LORD." And you forgave me! All my guilt is gone. PSALM 32:1-3, 5

DAY 12

A prayer about PASSION

When my passion for God has waned

LORD GOD,

My passion for following you has lessened. I find that my mind and heart are often focused on something else—any new thing in my life that seems fresh and exciting. I really don't want to move away from you; I want to be near you! Lord, I know that if what I'm most excited about is not what you want in my life, my passion for you will quickly die. Please help me. Give me the self-discipline to control my thoughts and help me to return my focus to you. I know that when I focus on you, I will again respond to you with joy. You will restore me.

You must continue to believe this truth and stand firmly in it. Don't drift away from the assurance you received when you heard the Good News. COLOSSIANS 1:23

DAY 13 *Prayerful Moment*

A prayer about LIFE'S DEMANDS
When life's demands seem overwhelming

MERCIFUL GOD,
The demands on my life seem impossible to deal with right now. The tasks are too hard, the burdens too much to bear, the schedule too full to manage. When demands pile up, may I always turn to you, my only source of help. Lord, please carry the burden for me or give me the strength to continue.

In my distress I cried out to the LORD; yes, I cried to my God for help. . . . My cry reached his ears. 2 SAMUEL 22:7

DAY 14 *Prayerful Moment*

A prayer about CHARACTER
When I find myself wanting to be a woman whom others admire

O LORD,
I confess that I sometimes put my emphasis on something that does not last—my outward appearance. I want others to admire me, but I know that outward beauty is not what will spur true admiration. Teach me that the most admirable qualities grow from having deep respect for you. I want to reflect your character, God. As I do that, may I develop the qualities that others can look up to.

Charm is deceptive, and beauty does not last; but a woman who fears the LORD will be greatly praised.
PROVERBS 31:30

DAY 15

A prayer for ADAPTABILITY
When I need to adapt to life's changes

RIGHTEOUS GOD,

I know that the ability to adapt goes hand in hand with trusting you. As I learn to trust that you love me and that you have the best plans for my life, I will be able to adjust willingly and quickly when the road of life takes a sudden sharp turn. Father, please help me to understand that I don't need to know all the details of your plan to obey it—I know your way is best, no matter where it takes me. Teach me to let go of the desire to control my life. May I move forward in faith and obedience, realizing that because you know the way, I don't have to.

It was by faith that Abraham obeyed when God called him to leave home and go to another land that God would give him as his inheritance. He went without knowing where he was going. And even when he reached the land God promised him, he lived there by faith—for he was like a foreigner, living in tents. HEBREWS 11:8-9

DAY 16

A prayer for when I'm OVERWHELMED
When I'm overwhelmed with life's struggles

LORD JESUS,

Right now I feel overwhelmed, defeated, powerless, out of control, and I don't see any way to overcome my circumstances. Life seems full of immense obstacles and opponents I will never be able to defeat. How can I escape? In desperation I can only cling to your promise that you have overcome the world. You are in control, and someday my problems will seem miniscule in the light of eternity and your great victory. You have also given me your Holy Spirit to help me overcome the obstacles and temptations in my life. Thank you, Lord. I know that on this earth I will never be free from trouble, but your Holy Spirit gives me the power to overcome it. Show me how to see the obstacles in my life as opportunities for you to show your power; then they will not seem so overwhelming. In your wisdom and grace, you can use the very hardships and weaknesses that frighten me as tools to help me overcome.

[Jesus said,] "I have told you all this so that you may have peace in me. Here on earth you will have many trials and sorrows. But take heart, because I have overcome the world."
JOHN 16:33

A prayer about DIFFERENCES
When I wonder how differences can be positive

LORD GOD,
Some of the people in my family, my workplace, and my neighborhood are not like me at all—we have such different tastes, personalities, abilities, and even worldviews. I usually think about such differences negatively, because it can be frustrating to try to understand people whose points of view are so dramatically different from my own. But now I'm trying to understand how differences can be a good thing; after all, in your infinite wisdom, you made light and darkness work together to form one day. You knew that both night and day are necessary—opposites united to create something that's greater than each on its own. Lord, please show me how I can be united with people who are different from me. Use our differences to accomplish something whole, something significant, and something pleasing to you. May we work together in a harmony that can come only because we follow the example of your Son, Jesus.

Live in harmony and peace. Then the God of love and peace will be with you. 2 CORINTHIANS 13:11

A prayer about LONELINESS
When I feel alone

HEAVENLY FATHER,

I feel so alone right now. Some of my relationships have failed, and it doesn't seem as if anyone understands me or cares about me. I want to give up on people altogether, but I know that will only cause me to feel sorry for myself and become even more discouraged. Father, I take comfort in the fact that you are always with me, even when I feel alone. Your Word tells me that you are thinking about me all the time! Help me to use this lonely time to rediscover your faithfulness—refresh me and fill my heart anew with hope and love. As you do, I know you will help me begin to reach out to others again. Cause me to take the focus off my lonely feelings and put it on another person's well-being. When I do, my loneliness will ease. Give me the courage to put myself in places where I can get to know new people—and perhaps even serve you at the same time. Thank you for your presence with me.

Those who know your name trust in you, for you, O LORD, do not abandon those who search for you. PSALM 9:10

DAY 19

A prayer about PRAYER
When I wonder if God always answers prayer

DEAR GOD,

Sometimes I wonder if you really answer prayer. So many of my prayers seem to remain unanswered, and I'm discouraged. Yet I cling to your Word, which clearly says that you hear your people. When I pray I know I want to receive a "yes" answer, but that may not be what you want for me. Please give me the humility to understand that you may sometimes say "no" or "wait—not now." Any loving parent sometimes gives these answers to a child, so I should also expect them from you, my heavenly Father. May I have faith to trust that you always answer based on what you know is best for me. Guard me from misinterpreting a seeming lack of response as your ignoring me or not caring about me; instead, give me the sensitivity to know when you are pointing me in a new direction. As I seek to understand how your answer is best, may I grow in spiritual wisdom.

I love the LORD because he hears my voice and my prayer for mercy. Because he bends down to listen, I will pray as long as I have breath! PSALM 116:1-2

DAY 20 *Prayerful Moment*

A prayer about HEAVEN
When I consider how the hope of heaven should affect my life

ETERNAL GOD,
My present life is but a blink of an eye when compared to the eternal life to come. Yet you have determined that how I live during my short time on earth will prepare me for heaven. May this truth give me purpose, perspective on my troubles, and anticipation for what you have planned for me in eternity.

Our present troubles are small and won't last very long. Yet they produce for us a glory that vastly outweighs them and will last forever! 2 CORINTHIANS 4:17

DAY 21 *Prayerful Moment*

A prayer about WORSHIP
When I want to express my love for God

FATHER,
I want to show my love for you through intentional worship. Too often when I'm with other believers, I mumble a few hymns, sit through a sermon, and go home. That's not true worship! I want to praise you with my whole being, body and soul. May I express my deepest devotion and affection for you through worship.

Give to the LORD the glory he deserves! Bring your offering and come into his presence. Worship the LORD in all his holy splendor. 1 CHRONICLES 16:29

DAY 22

A prayer about COMMUNITY

When I want to be a light to my community

LORD,

I want to be an example of your love to the people around me. I don't pretend that there's anything special about me, but your influence on my life can make me attractive to others. Help me to reflect your loving character in such a way that others will be drawn to me, and through me to you. Show me how to do that, whether it's by being a friendly neighbor, serving the needy in my community, making peace with difficult people, or treating others with fairness and respect. Through your power, make me a beacon of light that brightens the whole community with your transforming ways. I know I'll make mistakes, but I want to live my life in such a way that my neighbors will see that you are in me.

You are the light of the world—like a city on a hilltop that cannot be hidden. No one lights a lamp and then puts it under a basket. Instead, a lamp is placed on a stand, where it gives light to everyone in the house. In the same way, let your good deeds shine out for all to see, so that everyone will praise your heavenly Father. MATTHEW 5:14-16

A prayer about EMOTIONS
When I wonder what God thinks about emotions

LORD,

You have created me to be an emotional being, but sometimes others discourage me from expressing my feelings. Many people seem to think that our goal as Christians is to be stoic or tranquil at all times, never swaying from an even keel. However, the reality is that emotions are a good gift from you. After all, they're evidence that I am created in your image! When I read the Bible, I see that you displayed a whole range of emotions, including anger, sorrow, love, and zeal. Through the prophets, you cried out to the Israelites in anguish when they turned away from you, and you spoke passionately about your love for them when they turned back. It's clear that you don't want me to be an emotionless robot, but a person who loves what you love, hates what you hate, and rejoices in what brings you joy. Thank you for giving me emotions. Please continue to mold me so my emotions mirror your own.

Long ago the LORD said to Israel: "I have loved you, my people, with an everlasting love. With unfailing love I have drawn you to myself." JEREMIAH 31:3

A prayer about GRACE
When I marvel at God's grace

MERCIFUL GOD,

Grace is one of the richest words you have given us in the Bible. It's both a onetime act—the special favor you showed in giving me salvation through faith in Jesus—and a way of life—your ongoing work in me. I'm amazed when I think of all the blessings you've given me that I don't deserve, and the punishment for my sins that you've withheld even though that's what I do deserve. Words can't express my gratitude for your grace! As the song says, "Amazing grace! How sweet the sound that saved a wretch like me! I once was lost, but now am found; was blind, but now I see." My heart is moved to share your mercy with those around me because I want others to know the acceptance and freedom you offer. May I be faithful to extend your grace to everyone I meet.

God saved you by his grace when you believed. And you can't take credit for this; it is a gift from God. Salvation is not a reward for the good things we have done, so none of us can boast about it. EPHESIANS 2:8-9

DAY 25

A prayer about HOSPITALITY

When I want to make my home an inviting place

LORD GOD,

Your Word speaks highly of hospitality. It's not always easy for me to welcome people into my home, but when I do, I'm reflecting your character. You care for all people, and you have extended a warm invitation for us to join you in your heavenly home. Father, I tend to get caught up in details, such as how well my house is decorated, what I'm serving for dinner, or whether I have cleaned adequately before my guests arrive. Please help me to remember that those things are not nearly as important as the love I lavish on my guests. May I not be distracted by things that are really about me. Instead, may I focus on my guests, greeting them warmly and trying to meet their needs, whether that means serving food or drink, providing a place to stay overnight, or offering a listening ear or a sympathetic heart. Who knows what could come of my hospitality? Perhaps it will even be the way another person understands and accepts your invitation to join you in heaven.

Cheerfully share your home with those who need a meal or a place to stay. God has given each of you a gift from his great variety of spiritual gifts. Use them well to serve one another.

1 PETER 4:9-10

A prayer about QUIETNESS
When I want to hear God's voice

LORD,

I want to hear you and follow your leading. But often when I listen for you, I'm expecting you to speak through something big and obvious. Remind me that sometimes I must be still, quiet, and prepared in order to hear you speak. I need to spend time in your presence without noise and distractions. Help me to be calm, meditate on Scripture, and listen for you to speak to my heart and mind. Like the prophet Elijah, may I learn to recognize and obey your still, small voice.

"Go out and stand before me on the mountain," the LORD told [Elijah]. And as Elijah stood there, the LORD passed by, and a mighty windstorm hit the mountain. It was such a terrible blast that the rocks were torn loose, but the LORD was not in the wind. After the wind there was an earthquake, but the LORD was not in the earthquake. And after the earthquake there was a fire, but the LORD was not in the fire. And after the fire there was the sound of a gentle whisper. When Elijah heard it, he wrapped his face in his cloak and went out and stood at the entrance of the cave. And a voice said, "What are you doing here, Elijah?"

1 KINGS 19:11-13

DAY 27 *Prayerful Moment*

A prayer about the HEART
When I need an obedient heart

LORD,

Every farmer knows that you reap what you sow. That's why I'm asking you to plant a pure and obedient spirit within my heart so that my life will produce clean thoughts, actions, and motives. With your help, may I produce a harvest of righteousness.

You will always harvest what you plant. Those who live only to satisfy their own sinful nature will harvest decay and death. . . . But those who live to please the Spirit will harvest everlasting life from the Spirit. GALATIANS 6:7-8

DAY 28 *Prayerful Moment*

A prayer of PRAISE
When I long to praise God

O LORD,

You are the creator and sustainer of life. You are worthy of my highest praise! You made the heavens, placed the planets and stars in motion, and breathed life into every human being. Yet you desire a personal relationship with me! I am awed. I am overwhelmed by your greatness. Most mighty God, may I always respond to you with adoration, joy, and praise.

Great is the LORD! He is most worthy of praise! He is to be feared above all gods. The gods of other nations are mere idols, but the LORD made the heavens!

1 CHRONICLES 16:25-26

A prayer about DOUBT
When I need to overcome doubt

FATHER GOD,

I know that doubt can either be a trapdoor leading to fear or a doorway opening to confident faith. When I can't see your help but I choose to trust you anyway and you act, my faith is strengthened. You want me to express my faith in you before you respond—because if I wait until after you act, it's not really faith. So when you call me to a task, as you did with Gideon, I know I shouldn't be surprised when it seems that the obstacles are stacking up. You may be preparing to show me that you are the one coming to my rescue, that deliverance didn't come because of my own efforts. When Gideon's army dwindled to only a few soldiers, he realized that he was no longer in charge; only you could help him. You did, mightily, and your name was glorified throughout Israel! Teach me to realize that when I can't accomplish a job on my own, when I'm ready to give you the credit, and when even amid doubts I hold on to my belief that you have called me to do something for you, then I'll be in a position to see you work.

The LORD said to Gideon, "You have too many warriors with you. If I let all of you fight the Midianites, the Israelites will boast to me that they saved themselves by their own strength. . . . Bring them down to the spring, and I will test them to determine who will go with you and who will not." . . . The LORD told Gideon, "With these 300 men I will rescue you and give you victory over the Midianites. Send all the others home." JUDGES 7:2, 4, 7

A prayer about QUITTING
When I am tempted to quit

LORD GOD,
I'm in a very difficult situation, and I am wondering if it's time to quit. What should I do? There are no clear reasons to quit, and I believe you called me into this situation. So, Lord, let me be encouraged by the apostle Paul, who persevered through arrests, beatings, and persecution. He knew you had called him to share the gospel with the Gentiles, and nothing deterred him. May I have that same tenacity to keep on with the specific task to which you have called me. If I give up when it becomes difficult, I will miss the great blessing of reaching my goal and serving you. Help me to remember that just because you have asked me to do something doesn't mean it will be easy. The harder the road, the stronger I will become. I need endurance, Lord. Please give me the strength to keep going even when things get tough. Grant me the faith to follow your lead and move forward with confidence.

We are pressed on every side by troubles, but we are not crushed. We are perplexed, but not driven to despair. . . . We know that God, who raised the Lord Jesus, will also raise us with Jesus and present us to himself together with you. . . . That is why we never give up.
2 CORINTHIANS 4:8, 14, 16

A prayer about the CULTURE I live in
When I wonder how my culture is affecting me

FATHER GOD,

Just as the weather affects my life every day—influencing what I wear, what activities I choose to do, and even my mood—so the culture around me constantly affects me. It subtly influences my values, beliefs, and actions, and it pressures me to conform and fit in. Please open my eyes to the ways I am being changed by my culture. I never want to make choices that are disappointing to you. I know that my best defense against negative influences is to spend time in your Word, becoming ever more familiar with your ways. I need to keep my eyes fixed on your standard so I can see when I deviate from it. Lord, I invite you to challenge my worldview. Change the way I think about and respond to my culture. May I never be conformed to the world but instead be conformed to your image.

Don't copy the behavior and customs of this world, but let God transform you into a new person by changing the way you think. Then you will learn to know God's will for you, which is good and pleasing and perfect. ROMANS 12:2

DAY 32

A prayer about SELF-ESTEEM
When I'm struggling with insecurity

FATHER,

I struggle with insecurity, and often I think it's because I'm measuring my value by the wrong things. I compare myself to other women and worry about how I measure up in appearance, intelligence, or even popularity. Am I a better mother, wife, daughter, or friend than someone else? I evaluate myself all the time. Not only is it exhausting, but it makes me look at other women as competition instead of as people created in your image, deserving of love. That's not what you want for me. Rather, you want me to think of others as people created in your image, deserving of love. Teach me, Lord, that the only thing that matters—the only way to be secure—is to find my value as your creation. You say that I am one of your masterpieces! Your power within me can give me a healthy and confident self-esteem because, with you, I am capable of becoming far more than I could ever dream on my own.

We are God's masterpiece. He has created us anew in Christ Jesus, so we can do the good things he planned for us long ago.
EPHESIANS 2:10

A prayer about SURRENDER
When I surrender my life to God

HEAVENLY FATHER,

I want to surrender my life to you—to give up what I think is best and to do what you know is best. Help me, God, to put aside my self-fulfilling ambitions so that I can do the job you have for me. May your Holy Spirit live in me and through me. When I try to control my own life, I run into many problems. I struggle and I fall. So I give up control to you, knowing that you created me, love me, know me, and have a plan for me. I trust you with everything I have. When I stop grasping for what I want and release my life into your hands, I know I will begin to experience true freedom.

Christ's love controls us. Since we believe that Christ died for all, we also believe that we have all died to our old life. He died for everyone so that those who receive his new life will no longer live for themselves. Instead, they will live for Christ, who died and was raised for them.

2 CORINTHIANS 5:14-15

DAY 34 *Prayerful Moment*

A prayer about PERFECTION

When my perfectionism is hindering my relationship with God

LORD,

Sometimes my perfectionism keeps me from acting. I'm so worried about messing something up that I wait and wait for the perfect opportunity. But you don't ask for perfection. In fact, you love working through imperfect people and circumstances! Teach me, Lord, that all you ask is for me to follow you at every opportunity. You'll take care of the rest.

Even perfection has its limits, but your commands have no limit. PSALM 119:96

✓

DAY 35 *Prayerful Moment*

A prayer about COMPLACENCY

When I am dulled by complacency

LORD,

Just as the Israelites became spiritually complacent when they were not threatened by enemies, so I become complacent when things are going well. As much as I hate facing struggles in my life, I know that trials are what keep me spiritually sharp and fully dependent on you. Remind me that my health, relationships, financial stability, and other earthly blessings can vanish in an instant. You are my only security.

Lord, where do I put my hope? My only hope is in you. PSALM 39:7

✓ A prayer about FRIENDSHIP
When I wonder how I can be God's friend

LORD,

I'm amazed when I read in the Gospels that Jesus called his disciples friends. That means that you can call me *friend*, too, as incredible as that seems. What a blessing! But how can I be your friend? What kind of friend are you seeking? When I think about good friends, the qualities that come to mind are honesty, loyalty, and availability. Perhaps you appreciate those qualities too. Teach me to come to you openly and tell you all about my struggles and my successes. May I remain loyal to you and your Word and make myself available to spend quality time with you. As I confide in you and remain faithful to you, may our friendship deepen day by day. I am privileged to be called your friend.

[Jesus said,] "I no longer call you slaves, because a master doesn't confide in his slaves. Now you are my friends, since I have told you everything the Father told me."
JOHN 15:15

DAY 37

A prayer about SUCCESS

When I wonder if it's okay to seek success in this life

FATHER GOD,

I have ambitions to be successful in this world, but I wonder if that's okay. Is it wrong to desire the favor of my supervisors, prestige, more responsibility, or security in my financial situation? Sometimes these things come not because I'm actively seeking them but just because I'm working hard, serving others, and living with integrity, which are rewarded in the workplace. You ask me to do my work as if I'm laboring for you. Help me to make pleasing you my motivation, then rewards will not be my aim; but if they come, I can be grateful for your blessing. When I receive material blessings, may I never forget you, the one who gave them. Guard me from sacrificing spirituality for the sake of gaining worldly wealth. And help me always to remember that your standards are different from the world's. You measure success not by prestige, power, or possessions but by my motives, devotion, and commitment to you. Lord, in my work, my service, and my interactions with others, let my primary aim be to find success in your eyes.

Work willingly at whatever you do, as though you were working for the Lord rather than for people.

COLOSSIANS 3:23

A prayer about FATIGUE

When I am exhausted and need help to keep going

HEAVENLY FATHER,

You created me as a flesh-and-blood human being, and I'm grateful that you know my need for rest. Even Jesus, when he was on earth, understood the limitations of his body and took regular opportunities to be alone and rest. My life is so busy. It's full of good things, but if I don't pay attention to the health of my body and soul, I get so tired. Then I can't think clearly and I'm apt to do or say something I'll regret. Please renew my strength. I know that when I'm tired, I have an extra opportunity to experience your faithfulness. Refresh my heart as I come to you in praise, refresh my soul as I come to you in prayer, refresh my body as I come to you in solitude, and refresh my mind as I come to you in need. As I approach you, may I have a thankful heart and receive a renewed perspective. I love you, Lord. Thank you that I can draw strength from you and release my burdens into your hands.

He gives power to the weak and strength to the powerless. Even youths will become weak and tired, and young men will fall in exhaustion. But those who trust in the LORD will find new strength. They will soar high on wings like eagles. They will run and not grow weary. They will walk and not faint. ISAIAH 40:29-31

DAY 39

A prayer about the WILL OF GOD

When I want to know what God's will is for my life

HEAVENLY FATHER,

I want to follow your will for my life, but sometimes it seems so vague and difficult to know what that is. I wish you would give a clear sign to show me the way! But the truth is, in your Word you have already given me a whole set of directions that will keep me in your will. I want to do my best to follow your commands. You call me to worship you only, love my neighbors and enemies, use my spiritual gifts, tell the truth, refrain from coveting and stealing, be sexually pure, teach my children spiritual truths, avoid gossip, be generous, read your Word regularly, let the Holy Spirit control my life—and other instructions for healthy, godly living. What more direction do I need? Please give me the willingness and self-discipline I need to live according to the guidance you have set forth in the Scriptures. Then I know I will be right where I want to be: in the center of your will.

Your word is a lamp to guide my feet and a light for my path.

PSALM 119:105

DAY 40

A prayer about HONESTY
When I seek to live an honest life

LORD,

I want to be completely trustworthy, honest in even the little things. It's sometimes tempting to cut corners and cheat on small details, but I know doing that is a slippery slope that may make it difficult for me to be honest when bigger things are at stake. Help me always to remember that even if no one else is watching, you see. You know my character, Lord—my strengths and weaknesses. I need you to work in my heart as I seek to become a woman of complete integrity. Give me the discipline to build my life with the bricks of honesty so that I may have a strong foundation upon which to act with integrity when I encounter greater challenges and responsibilities. May my life always be governed by your standards of fairness and justice.

Who may climb the mountain of the LORD? Who may stand in his holy place? Only those whose hands and hearts are pure, who do not worship idols and never tell lies. They will receive the LORD's blessing and have a right relationship with God their savior. PSALM 24:3-5

DAY 41 *Prayerful Moment*

✓ A prayer about PEACE
When I'm in conflict with someone

FATHER,
A relationship in my life is filled with tension, and I want to bring peace. Please help me to remember that peace is not the absence of conflict; rather, it's having confident assurance in the middle of conflict. Only you can give me that assurance, Lord. Teach me to deal with disagreements well and to pursue peace, even when it's hard work. I know that you will bless me when I bring your peace to others.

God blesses those who work for peace, for they will be called the children of God. MATTHEW 5:9

✓ # DAY 42 *Prayerful Moment*

A prayer about SERVICE
When I want to serve God with joy

HEAVENLY FATHER,
Being your servant is not a dull obligation but a great privilege. Sometimes I fall into the trap of rote service, doing things just because they have to be done. But when I remember the *why* behind my service—that it's for your glory and the furthering of your Kingdom—then my attitude is transformed. May I always serve you joyfully, with gratitude for the opportunity and for the ability to show my devotion to you.

Serve the LORD with reverent fear, and rejoice with trembling.
PSALM 2:11

A prayer about COMMUNICATION
When I want to improve my communication

LORD GOD,
Thank you that we have the gift of communication, which helps us connect with one another in a deeper way. I'm blessed by opportunities to share my thoughts and experiences with others. It's easy for me to talk, but it's not always easy for me to say exactly what I mean in a way that's kind and effective. And often I shy away from any conversation that might involve conflict. Please give me the courage to be honest as I talk with my family, my coworkers, and my friends. Help me to keep the lines of communication open, even when a conversation is awkward or hard. Teach me to use words that are full of grace and truth. May I remember the importance of affirmation and find ways to encourage others with my words each day.

Don't use foul or abusive language. Let everything you say be good and helpful, so that your words will be an encouragement to those who hear them. EPHESIANS 4:29

DAY 44

A prayer about HEALTH
When I wonder if God cares about my physical health

O LORD,

I know that my spiritual health is important to you, even though I sometimes wonder whether you care about my physical health. But then I remember how Jesus cared for the physical well-being of the people around him, and I trust that you care for my physical well-being, too. My body is your temple, and I need to treat it with respect. Teach me to care diligently for the body you have given me even as I remember that the benefits of physical fitness last only for this earthly life, while the benefits of spiritual fitness last for eternity. I know that the two are intertwined. My spiritual disciplines—worship, prayer, obedience to your Word—have a profound impact on my physical life, and my physical habits—such as exercise and nutrition—can influence my spiritual life. Please show me the right balance, and help me to remember that your presence in me should affect all aspects of my life.

Don't you realize that your body is the temple of the Holy Spirit, who lives in you and was given to you by God? You do not belong to yourself, for God bought you with a high price. So you must honor God with your body.

1 CORINTHIANS 6:19-20

DAY 45

✓ A prayer for HUMILITY
When I'm struggling with pride

HEAVENLY FATHER,
Pride has tripped me up today. Whenever I think I'm invulnerable to sin, I'm giving the devil the key to my heart and setting myself up for a fall. Forgive me for my pride, Lord. May I always have the humility to recognize my own failures and be sorrowful over my sin. I need you desperately, and I want to give you my whole heart. Open me up to be used for your purposes—not because I am especially gifted but because you can work through me. When I try on my own to seem important, I run into trouble. But you promise that when I humble myself before you, you will lift me up.

[God] gives us even more grace to stand against such evil desires. As the Scriptures say, "God opposes the proud but favors the humble." So humble yourselves before God. Resist the devil, and he will flee from you. Come close to God, and God will come close to you. Wash your hands, you sinners; purify your hearts, for your loyalty is divided between God and the world. Let there be tears for what you have done. . . . Humble yourselves before the Lord, and he will lift you up in honor. JAMES 4:6-10

A prayer about COMMITMENT
When I want to strengthen my commitment to God

LORD JESUS,

My family is at the center of so much that I do, and they are a blessing to me. So I struggle when I read your strong words telling your disciples to hate even their families and their own lives in comparison with you. But I think the key is that you want us to see that commitment to you is exclusive and costly. You must become the central and dominating commitment of my life, and I must consider all other loves—even my family—in light of that. Show me what that means for me. Certainly I need to make financial decisions based on biblical principles, instead of just buying what I want. Perhaps you might lead me to make sacrifices to help needy people, even if it puts additional strain on my own family. Lord, too often my commitment to you is diluted by everything else in my life. Help me to evaluate everything by asking, "Is this worthy of my time and affection in light of my complete devotion to you?"

[Jesus said,] "If you want to be my disciple, you must hate everyone else by comparison—your father and mother, wife and children, brothers and sisters—yes, even your own life. Otherwise, you cannot be my disciple. And if you do not carry your own cross and follow me, you cannot be my disciple. But don't begin until you count the cost."

LUKE 14:26-28

✓ A prayer about LOYALTY

When I want to express true friendship through loyalty

LOVING GOD,

I'm thankful for my friendships with other women. It's easy to be a friend when things are going well, but I don't want to be a fair-weather friend, leaving when I'm no longer benefiting from the relationship. I know that true friendship is characterized by loyalty. Teach me to be available to my friends even—or especially—in times of their distress or personal struggle. Help me to follow the wonderful example of Ruth, whose loyalty and commitment to Naomi went far beyond what was expected of her. I pray that my loyalty to the friends you have given me will pass the test of adversity. May my faithfulness to friends in times of trouble be an encouragement that will give them a glimpse of your eternal faithfulness.

[The women] wept together, and Orpah kissed her mother-in-law good-bye. But Ruth clung tightly to Naomi. "Look," Naomi said to her, "your sister-in-law has gone back to her people and to her gods. You should do the same." But Ruth replied, "Don't ask me to leave you and turn back. Wherever you go, I will go; wherever you live, I will live. Your people will be my people, and your God will be my God."

RUTH 1:14-16

DAY 48 *Prayerful Moment*

A prayer about HOPE
When I need hope to get me through a tough time

GOD OF HOPE,
Everything seems to be falling apart right now. I'm clinging to the fact that you keep your word. You promise that in heaven all my problems and suffering will be over. Never again will I grieve or be discouraged! May that hope for the future encourage me and get me through my present struggles.

Let us hold tightly without wavering to the hope we affirm, for God can be trusted to keep his promise.
HEBREWS 10:23

DAY 49 *Prayerful Moment*

A prayer about THANKFULNESS
When I want to cultivate a thankful heart

LORD GOD,
I want to have a thankful heart. I know the best way to cultivate thankfulness is simply to give thanks regularly. Help me to set aside time every day for gratitude. No matter what my feelings are at the moment, may I make a mental list of all your blessings and thank you for them. I trust that as I give thanks I will begin to develop more and more gratitude—and that will keep my struggles in perspective.

Be thankful in all circumstances, for this is God's will for you who belong to Christ Jesus.
1 THESSALONIANS 5:18

A prayer about ETERNITY
When I wonder what eternal life will be like

ALMIGHTY GOD,
I am amazed when I consider eternity. I can't wrap my mind around the concept of anything lasting forever, but I believe your Word. I'm thankful that eternity won't be merely an extension of my life here on earth, where I suffer, grieve, and hurt. You promise something new. I praise you because you will restore this earth to the way you once created it—a beautiful place with no sin, sorrow, or pain. How I look forward to a new earth that is better than this one in every way! I know I will have plenty of fulfilling and purposeful things to do. Best of all, I will be in your presence and forever filled with joy.

Look, God's home is now among his people! He will live with them, and they will be his people. God himself will be with them. He will wipe every tear from their eyes, and there will be no more death or sorrow or crying or pain. All these things are gone forever. REVELATION 21:3-4

✓ A prayer about RECONCILIATION

When I ponder the importance of being at peace with others

LORD GOD,

Reconciliation is at the heart of what it means to follow you. After all, Jesus suffered the agony of the cross to redeem sinful humans—including me—and close the gap between us and God. Thank you, Lord! Impress on my heart that this restoration doesn't end there; it also extends to my relationships with those around me. In fact, your Word tells me that my reconciliation with you is a picture of how I am to be reconciled with others. You care about harmony among people so much that you say in the Bible that living with an unresolved conflict can actually hinder my relationship with you. I don't want that, Lord. Search my heart and show me anyone in my life with whom you want me to pursue reconciliation. May I be willing to take the first step in resolving past conflicts, and as I go forward, teach me to live in peace with those around me.

If you are presenting a sacrifice at the altar in the Temple and you suddenly remember that someone has something against you, leave your sacrifice there at the altar. Go and be reconciled to that person. Then come and offer your sacrifice to God. MATTHEW 5:23-24

A prayer about WORTH
When I wonder if I am worthy

LORD GOD,
I struggle to see myself accurately. At some moments I fail to see my faults, and at other times I fail to see my value. Impress on my heart that you love me for who I am, not because of what I do for you. Psalm 139 tells me that you loved me before I made my first mistake, before I uttered my first word, and even before I took my first breath! Your love for me is an eternal thread woven through my life and is strengthened through the life, death, and resurrection of Jesus on my behalf. That kind of love amazes me. How can I not be encouraged? When I doubt my worth, may I never forget that you have made me worthy—through the precious blood of Christ.

If God is for us, who can ever be against us? Since he did not spare even his own Son but gave him up for us all, won't he also give us everything else? Who dares accuse us whom God has chosen for his own? No one—for God himself has given us right standing with himself. ROMANS 8:31-33

✓ ## A prayer about DISCOURAGEMENT
When I'm feeling discouraged and sorry for myself

LOVING GOD,

I need some encouragement right now. I feel as though I am the only one who is going through troubles, and I'm feeling sorry for myself. Please give me the insight to realize that other people around me are struggling too—I'm not being singled out. Now and anytime I feel discouraged, may my response always be to come to you in prayer. I'm grateful that you invite me to talk to you, to be honest with you, and to share my burdens with you. I know I'm never alone. You are near and ready to help; in fact, your Word says that you will fight on my behalf, just as you did for the Israelites when they were fleeing from their Egyptian captors. All I have to do is stand still and watch you work. Help me to trust in you, never losing sight of your great love for me. You are the great encourager, and I rest in you.

Moses told the people, "Don't be afraid. Just stand still and watch the LORD rescue you today. The Egyptians you see today will never be seen again. The LORD himself will fight for you. Just stay calm." EXODUS 14:13-14

✓ ## A prayer about PLANS

When I want my plans to be in line with God's will

HEAVENLY FATHER,

I love to make plans for the future—for myself, my family, my home, my work. You have created me with this desire to be forward thinking and purposeful, yet I must always acknowledge that your plans take precedence over mine. May I be mindful of your revealed plans laid out in the Bible, as well as your specific plan for me. You created me with a unique purpose, but you don't always make that purpose crystal clear. The truth is, if you were to reveal everything, I might not feel that I needed your guidance anymore. Please give me the courage to walk step-by-step with you in faith, trusting that you will show me just enough of your plan to help me take the next step. Give me the discipline to read your Word and obey it, for that is the best way to discover your plans for me. Teach me to keep my heart turned toward you so that I may be sensitive to your leading. Then I can move forward with confidence, knowing that someday I will look back and see your divine guidance in my life.

"I know the plans I have for you," says the LORD. *"They are plans for good and not for disaster, to give you a future and a hope."* JEREMIAH 29:11

DAY 55 *Prayerful Moment*

A prayer about FREEDOM
When I desire true freedom

LORD GOD,
It's easy for me to define *freedom* as being able to do whatever I want. But I've tried that and it only led me back into slavery. I want genuine freedom, and the only way I will experience it is if I embrace the truth about my own neediness and your provision. I need you desperately. Overcome my sinful inclinations with your holiness, Lord. May I find true freedom when you fill my life with the goodness and fullness of your liberating love.

You will know the truth, and the truth will set you free.
JOHN 8:32

DAY 56 *Prayerful Moment*

A prayer about CONFIDENCE
When I want to be confident in God

LORD JESUS,
I need a reminder today that true confidence doesn't come from my physical circumstances, such as how I look, where I live, or what I achieve. Teach me instead that genuine confidence comes from the inner assurance that you are by my side, making your wisdom and power available to me and working out your purpose for my life. Thank you, Lord, for being the source of my confidence.

I can do everything through Christ, who gives me strength.
PHILIPPIANS 4:13

A prayer about TEAMWORK
When I need to work with others

FATHER GOD,
Often I resist working with others because it seems so much easier just to do everything by myself. But then I complain that I'm overworked! Help me to recognize the immeasurable value others can bring to the projects I'm involved in. Give me the humility to realize that not everything has to be done the way I would do it; my way is not always best. As I welcome others' input, may I appreciate their insight and creativity. You have created people to work with one another, encourage one another, and sharpen one another. I know that we are rarely at our best alone, so please teach me to embrace the concept of teamwork.

Two people are better off than one, for they can help each other succeed. If one person falls, the other can reach out and help. But someone who falls alone is in real trouble. . . . A person standing alone can be attacked and defeated, but two can stand back-to-back and conquer. Three are even better, for a triple-braided cord is not easily broken.
ECCLESIASTES 4:9-10, 12

A prayer about COMPASSION

When I struggle to reflect Christ's compassion

LORD JESUS,

Today my heart is hard. I see the needs around me, but they're not penetrating my heart. I find myself walking by hurting people, unable or unwilling to enter into their struggles. What is wrong? I know I'm too focused on myself—sometimes so much so that I can't see beyond my problems to others' pain. I keep myself at a distance from anyone who might disturb my equilibrium. Yet I'm afraid that if I keep going this way, I'll be in danger of developing a heart of stone that's unresponsive to you or to others. I don't want that, Lord. I want to love others as you love me. Please work in me; transform me. Stir up compassion for others that will melt my hard heart and compel me to action. I want to be your hands and feet in the world, sharing your love with those around me.

[Jesus said,] "I am giving you a new commandment: Love each other. Just as I have loved you, you should love each other. Your love for one another will prove to the world that you are my disciples." JOHN 13:34-35

✓ ## A prayer about DISCIPLINE
When God disciplines me

LORD GOD,

You call me your child, and I am so grateful that you are my heavenly Father. You love me as a parent—and you also sometimes discipline me as a parent would a child. Help me to remember that your discipline is an act of love. Its aim is to keep me from damaging my relationships and to make me into the person you created me to be. You want me to build good character and habits and teach me right from wrong, and I want that too. I know that, left to myself, I would always tend to move away from you and toward sin. Protect me from that, Lord. And keep me from being selfish and immature. May I respond to your discipline with humility, not with rebellion or anger, willing to learn and change. Shape me in your image, and remind me why obedience to you is always best. I know that whatever happens, I never have to doubt your overwhelming love for me.

No discipline is enjoyable while it is happening—it's painful! But afterward there will be a peaceful harvest of right living for those who are trained in this way. HEBREWS 12:11

DAY 60

✓ A prayer about CRISIS
When I don't know what to pray

LORD GOD,
I'm struggling in a time of crisis right now, and my thoughts are racing. I desperately need your help, but I don't know how to pray. I thank you that I don't have to ask you to be with me—you already are. You have said that you will never leave me or forsake me, no matter what happens in this world, and I cling to that promise. Help me, Lord, to recognize your presence and have the humility and discernment to accept your aid. Guide me toward peace and hope. Remind me of your promise to someday bring me to heaven, where all trouble, sickness, and pain will end forever. Calm my panic and bring peace to my mind and heart. May I be mindful of your loving presence today and always.

God is our refuge and strength, always ready to help in times of trouble. So we will not fear when earthquakes come and the mountains crumble into the sea. Let the oceans roar and foam. Let the mountains tremble as the waters surge!
PSALM 46:1-3

DAY 61

A prayer about STRENGTHS AND WEAKNESSES

When I wonder how God can use my strengths and weaknesses

FATHER GOD,

I know that people are not always what they seem. A petite woman might be an incredible endurance runner. A bodybuilder might have a weakness for drugs or alcohol. Sometimes what appears weak is strong beneath the surface, and what seems strong is actually weak. Help me to remember that external appearance is not a good indicator of internal spiritual strength. That's true for those around me, but it's also true for me. As I mature in my relationship with you, may I learn to recognize both my weaknesses and my strengths. I admit my weaknesses with humility, because your Word tells me that you call out the best in me when you work through my weaknesses. That's when your strength is shown most clearly. May I always rely on you to use both my strengths and weaknesses as I serve and glorify you. Then I will be truly strong.

Each time [the Lord] said, "My grace is all you need. My power works best in weakness." So now I am glad to boast about my weaknesses, so that the power of Christ can work through me. 2 CORINTHIANS 12:9

DAY 62 *Prayerful Moment*

A prayer about BUSYNESS
When I am too busy with unimportant things

DEAR LORD,
I want to be productive for your Kingdom, but so often I feel myself caught up in empty busyness. I'm rushing here and there; though many of the things I'm doing are good, I'm neglecting you and feeling that I have nothing left to give. Impress on my heart that my primary purpose is to know you and become more like you. Everything else will flow from that. My time is limited, Lord, so help me to make the most of the time you've given me.

Teach us to realize the brevity of life, so that we may grow in wisdom. PSALM 90:12

DAY 63 *Prayerful Moment*

A prayer about ENCOURAGING OTHERS
When I want to be an encourager

HEAVENLY FATHER,
You command me through your Word to build up other believers as a means of boosting their faith and strengthening the church. Please open my eyes to see the opportunities you give me to encourage others through a kind smile, affirming words, or simple help. May I be faithful in following through when you prompt me. I pray that these encounters will allow others to feel your rich love for them.

We should help others do what is right and build them up in the Lord. ROMANS 15:2

DAY 64

A prayer about OPPORTUNITIES

When I want to make the most of the opportunities that come my way

FATHER GOD,

I believe that you are sovereign and that you can work in all circumstances. So when I sense that you are presenting an opportunity for me to participate in your plan, I need to respond with bold action. I don't want to waste the opportunities you set before me or want my life to be defined by regret over opportunities I missed. Please give me the courage to respond quickly to what you place in front of me and the discipline to work hard to make the most of it. I want to be available to you, so I pray for the flexibility to be willing to change my plans when you present a new opportunity. I am amazed when I think that you might use me! Help me to keep my eyes open for whatever you will bring my way.

We must quickly carry out the tasks assigned us by the one who sent us. The night is coming, and then no one can work.
JOHN 9:4

DAY 65

A prayer about WISDOM

When I want to learn to be wise

HEAVENLY FATHER,

The world around me values intelligence more than wisdom, but your Word tells me that wisdom is far more important. I can work to gain more education and develop my intellect, but being intelligent doesn't guarantee that I'll have a fulfilled, balanced, or productive life. Success in relationships, fulfillment of my life's purpose, and spiritual maturity are all far more dependent on wisdom than on intellect. Wisdom comes only from you, so I turn to you for what I need to navigate through life successfully. As I grow in my knowledge of you and my respect for your commands, I will also grow in wisdom. Reveal your wisdom to me as I read the Bible. May I always have a humble and teachable heart so that I can absorb what you say. As I encounter different experiences, I pray that I will learn to link them with the truths of Scripture so that wisdom will flourish in my life. May I never mistake facts or head knowledge for true wisdom. Instead, I ask you to transform my knowledge into discernment and commonsense action. I want to be wise and reflect you, the creator of all knowledge and the fount of all wisdom.

Fear of the LORD is the foundation of true wisdom. All who obey his commandments will grow in wisdom.

PSALM 111:10

A prayer about PLEASURE

When I think about what brings me true pleasure

LORD,

I love to gather with friends, family, or other believers to celebrate! It's a blessing to enjoy food together and to express thanksgiving for your goodness and love. Thank you for allowing me to take pleasure in these good gifts from you. Just as I enjoy watching my family appreciate something special I prepared for them, I know you take pleasure in watching your children enjoy your blessings. At the same time, I read in your Word that the very best kind of pleasure is delighting in doing what you want. Your way is right and good and it brings life. You are pleased when I follow it, because you want the best for me. May I always find pleasure in obedience, Lord. When I do, I will be enjoying life as you intended me to enjoy it—to the fullest!

Oh, the joys of those who do not follow the advice of the wicked, or stand around with sinners, or join in with mockers. But they delight in the law of the LORD, meditating on it day and night. They are like trees planted along the riverbank, bearing fruit each season. Their leaves never wither, and they prosper in all they do. PSALM 1:1-3

A prayer about being OVERWHELMED
When I'm overcome by obstacles

HOLY GOD,

Your power is working for me, no matter how many enemies are against me. This truth gives me great encouragement! I see so many examples in your Word. You used the shepherd boy David to overcome the powerful Goliath. You used Gideon's three hundred soldiers to defeat the vast armies of Midian. You used a simple peasant girl to bear your Son. And you used twelve disciples to establish the worldwide church. If you can do all that, it's clear you can work through even my weaknesses and limitations. I'm so thankful that I don't have to be strong or smart or beautiful for you to do great things through me. All you ask is that I obey you. Thank you for the reassurance that I don't need to worry about the obstacles in front of me because I don't have to handle them—you will make a way. May I trust you and follow you always so that you may work in me.

Each one of you will put to flight a thousand of the enemy, for the LORD your God fights for you, just as he has promised.
JOSHUA 23:10

DAY 68

✓ A prayer about LOSS
When I have lost someone I love

COMPASSIONATE GOD,
I have lost someone I love, and I am overcome with grief. But one thing that brings me comfort is the example, recorded in your Word, of Jesus weeping over the death of Lazarus. Even though he knew that Lazarus would shortly be raised from the dead, Jesus still grieved over the terrible separation that death brings. It tears apart families and friends, and even though the fabric of our lives will heal, our lives will never be the same. Thank you for showing me that it's okay to grieve, to express the pain I'm feeling. Give me the patience to move through the process as slowly as I need to. And may I always remember that I grieve with hope, as one who knows you. I have the assurance of your love and the hope of eternal life. I praise you for the comforting promise that one day I will be with you in heaven, where all grief will be gone forever.

"Where have you put [Lazarus]?" [Jesus] asked them. They told him, "Lord, come and see." Then Jesus wept. The people who were standing nearby said, "See how much he loved him!" JOHN 11:34-36

DAY 69 *Prayerful Moment*

✓ **A prayer about MUSIC**
When I praise God through music

HEAVENLY FATHER,
The beauty of music testifies to your glory and majesty. While the lyrics I sing direct my mind toward you, the melody touches my heart in a way that simple words cannot. Thank you for music, which gives me a glimpse into your awesome, creative beauty. As I sing hymns and songs, may I worship in a meaningful way, expressing my gratitude and praise to you.

Praise the LORD! How good to sing praises to our God! How delightful and how fitting! PSALM 147:1

✓ DAY 70 *Prayerful Moment*

A prayer about CHURCH
When I worship with other believers

TRIUNE GOD,
How amazing that your Spirit lives in the heart of every believer! Moreover, your Word tells me that you live in the community of the church. When believers gather together, you are present in a special way. Participating with other Christians in worship is much more meaningful than worshiping by myself. Thank you for my church! As we meet together this week, may we worship in spirit and in truth.

[Jesus said,] "Where two or three gather together as my followers, I am there among them." MATTHEW 18:20

DAY 71

A prayer about GOSSIP
When I'm tempted to gossip

FATHER,
I have to confess that it can be fun to gossip. I love to be in on the latest news, and I enjoy connecting with others in conversation. But I know that gossip does not honor you. It's based on rumors, not facts, and it often damages someone's reputation rather than building it up. When I gossip, I feel myself judging others and becoming increasingly critical. That's not what I want, Lord. Please help me as I try to stop my gossip habit. I know that if I don't add fuel, the fire will go out. When I'm with others who are speaking hurtful rumors, prompt me to change the subject or say something kind about the person who's the target of the rumors. I pray that the compassionate words I say might allow your grace to break through to those around me and perhaps even reach the ears of those I defend. Guard my lips and cause me to speak words of healing instead of hurt.

The Scriptures say, "If you want to enjoy life and see many happy days, keep your tongue from speaking evil and your lips from telling lies." 1 PETER 3:10

A prayer about PRIORITIES

When I wonder how to set the right priorities

O LORD,

My life often skips from one "urgent" interruption to another. And all the while I keep missing what is really important. I need your wisdom to figure out what things matter most in life. How can I distinguish true priorities from false ones? I know that often I confuse what's urgent—such as a ringing phone or a pressing deadline—with what's important—such as a deep spiritual conversation with a friend, an opportunity to read a Bible story with my child, or a quiet moment in prayer. I need your help, Lord, to set my priorities at the start of every day. Guard me from letting everyone else decide what my day should look like; that's between you and me, and I need to decide that prayerfully with your help. As I make time with you the first priority of each day, grant me your perspective on the rest of my activities. Amid the busyness and clamor of the frequent interruptions I face, keep me calm and focused on the things that are really important—the things that will last forever.

Seek the Kingdom of God above all else, and live righteously, and he will give you everything you need.

MATTHEW 6:33

A prayer about CHOICES
When I need help making a decision

DEAR LORD,

Every day I face new choices, and I'm not always sure what to do. Sometimes I feel paralyzed by having so many options because I wonder if there really is just one right one. But I know that you don't want me to remain immobile, full of fear that I might make the wrong decision. No, you have set me free to serve you. Your Word makes it clear that the choices that will always be right are to honor you and to obey your instructions. This will without fail put me in the center of your will, and that's where I want to be! Lord, as I make difficult decisions, help me to seek your wisdom by reading your Word, searching for your guidance through prayer, and obtaining advice from godly counselors. When I put you ahead of everything and everyone else, I will be choosing to serve you—and that's a choice that will never be wrong.

Love the LORD your God, walk in all his ways, obey his commands, hold firmly to him, and serve him with all your heart and all your soul. JOSHUA 22:5

✓ A prayer about SERVICE

When I wonder what attitudes are necessary for serving God

LORD GOD,

With my whole heart, I want to serve you. As I do, fill me with joy and reverent awe because then I will remember whom I am serving. Grant me a strong desire to please you and obey your Word because that will give me the motivation to do my best. May I always be devoted to you, even willing to sacrifice some of my own comforts and desires in order to effectively reach out to those who need you. Fill my heart with genuine love for you, and may it spill over to others, enabling me to serve them. I know that if I'm focused primarily on my own desires, I won't be effective at helping others. Please work in my heart, Lord, so that I may have sincere love, genuine selflessness, and the self-discipline to put others first.

You have been called to live in freedom, my brothers and sisters. But don't use your freedom to satisfy your sinful nature. Instead, use your freedom to serve one another in love.

GALATIANS 5:13

A prayer about GOD'S HAND
When I need a reminder that God can do anything

ALMIGHTY GOD,
Your Word is filled with stories of the impossible: a flood covers the earth, a sea is parted so people can walk through it, the sun keeps shining until a battle can be won, a man survives three days in the belly of a fish, a virgin gives birth to a baby boy. If I didn't believe that you exist, these stories would defy all logic. But because I believe you are the creator of all things, I also believe that you can alter what you created. You can break natural law to cause something supernatural to happen. Your hand can do the impossible! O Lord, give me the faith to understand that what I see with my eyes is not all there is. Teach me to recognize and appreciate the impossible things you accomplish for me and around me each day. The most amazing of all is the miracle of redemption through Jesus. You specialize in doing what, from a human perspective, is impossible. When I reach the end of my abilities, may I always remember that this is just the beginning of yours.

[People asked,] "Then who in the world can be saved?" [Jesus] replied, "What is impossible for people is possible with God." LUKE 18:26-27

DAY 76 *Prayerful Moment*

✓ A prayer about being an INFLUENCE
When I want my life to help other people see God

DEAR LORD,
Help me to be obedient to you so that I might develop the character and integrity that will draw others to you. I want to live in such a way that I plant seeds of faith in the lives of people around me. I may never see how my life impacts others, but you will care for and nourish the seeds I plant, and perhaps some will grow into saving faith with you.

I planted the seed in your hearts, and Apollos watered it, but it was God who made it grow. 1 CORINTHIANS 3:6

✓ DAY 77 *Prayerful Moment*

A prayer about UNITY
When I wonder if true unity is possible

LORD,
I want to live in unity with my family and my church, but we as individuals are so different from one another! Help me to remember that unity is not about everyone agreeing. Teach me, Lord, how to celebrate the differences you have created. As I develop relationships, may I learn how to take different opinions and direct them toward a shared purpose. Even when I disagree with others on the details, please show us how to unite around the goal of serving you.

Make every effort to keep yourselves united in the Spirit, binding yourselves together with peace. EPHESIANS 4:3

A prayer about POTENTIAL
When I want to fulfill my God-given potential

LORD,

You have created me in your image, which means I can be a reflection of your marvelous characteristics. How amazing! I don't want to waste that potential. I have faith in you, Lord; I know that you are the only one who can complete what you have started. Help me to give you control of my life. Thank you that your Holy Spirit lives in my heart and helps me to reach the spiritual potential for which I was created. Work in me as only you can so that I may reflect your holiness and use my spiritual gifts to help others.

Because of the privilege and authority God has given me, I give each of you this warning: Don't think you are better than you really are. Be honest in your evaluation of yourselves, measuring yourselves by the faith God has given us.
ROMANS 12:3

DAY 79

A prayer about CONTENTMENT
When I'm not content

LORD,

I realize today that I've allowed discontentment to creep into my heart. Sometimes this feeling comes because I permit my present troubles to overshadow your past blessings. Other times it's the opposite: I feel dissatisfied because I'm stuck in the past, forgetting the blessings of today. Too often I compare myself to others and their possessions, and then I confuse my wants with my needs. O Lord, I need your help to regain the joy I once had—in life, in you, in my relationships with others. Teach me to keep my focus on you. Show me how to discipline my mind to find the good in every situation and to be thankful for my blessings. Then I will be content, trusting in you to provide for my every need.

True godliness with contentment is itself great wealth. After all, we brought nothing with us when we came into the world, and we can't take anything with us when we leave it. So if we have enough food and clothing, let us be content.
1 TIMOTHY 6:6-8

DAY 80

A prayer about BURNOUT

When I'm feeling overwhelmed and burned out

HEAVENLY FATHER,

Today I feel exhausted and unable to push on. I've been under a lot of stress, and I'm tapped out emotionally, mentally, physically, and spiritually. I wish the world would stop for just a few hours so I could take a break and rest before jumping back in! I can't make the world stop, but I can set aside my worries for a few moments and rest in your presence. Forgive me for neglecting my time with you, Lord. Please refresh me and strengthen me. Bless me with your peace, protection, and love. Help me to focus on the promises in your Word. When I remember who you are, I'll be refreshed, more calm, and better able to sort out my own priorities.

Jesus said, "Come to me, all of you who are weary and carry heavy burdens, and I will give you rest. Take my yoke upon you. Let me teach you, because I am humble and gentle at heart, and you will find rest for your souls. For my yoke is easy to bear, and the burden I give you is light."

MATTHEW 11:28-30

DAY 81

✓ ## A prayer about TITHING
When I wonder if tithing is really necessary

LORD GOD,

I want to support your work, but it's difficult to discipline myself to tithe. Sometimes I dismiss tithing as an out-of-date religious law, but I know that's not true. Your Word has a lot to say about giving. I know that, symbolically, giving the first part of my earnings to you demonstrates that you are my number one priority and that I am grateful for the blessings you have given me. I want to show my commitment to your work and honor you for your provision and faithfulness to me. Help me to develop the self-discipline to maintain a habit of regular tithing. May I give before I spend—that will keep you at the top of my priority list. I know that tithing will also give me the right perspective on the rest of my income. It's actually all yours, Lord. Teach me not to ask, "How much of 'my' money do I need to give to you?" but to ask instead, "How much of your money should I keep?" May I become a cheerful giver, one who feels privileged to support other believers, those in need, and the work of spreading your gospel.

You must each decide in your heart how much to give. And don't give reluctantly or in response to pressure. "For God loves a person who gives cheerfully."

2 CORINTHIANS 9:7

A prayer about TEMPTATION
When I need to resist temptation

LORD GOD,

I'm often tempted to sin. I know that's part of being human; after all, even Jesus faced temptation when he was on earth. But I want to do everything I can to keep from succumbing. Help me, Lord, to work to strengthen my faith *before* temptation comes. I'm determined to stand firm in my commitment to you, but I need your help to keep that commitment. Show me when I need to avoid areas of temptation or even to physically flee from compromising situations. Keep me aware that Satan will strike where I am weakest, so help me to recognize where I am vulnerable. Keep me alert, watching for temptation and praying for the strength to resist it. Then when it does come, I will be well prepared to withstand it.

The temptations in your life are no different from what others experience. And God is faithful. He will not allow the temptation to be more than you can stand. When you are tempted, he will show you a way out so that you can endure.

1 CORINTHIANS 10:13

DAY 83 *Prayerful Moment*

✓ A prayer about GOD'S PROMISES

When I am thankful for God's trustworthy promises

LORD,

You didn't just create truth; you *are* truth. You cannot lie! Your words are completely dependable. As I read your Word, I am amazed at all the wonderful things you have in store for me. You have promised salvation to those who confess Christ as Lord. You have promised an eternal future in heaven with you. You have promised your everlasting love. I praise you, Lord, for your trustworthy promises.

God has given both his promise and his oath. These two things are unchangeable because it is impossible for God to lie.
HEBREWS 6:18

✓ DAY 84 *Prayerful Moment*

A prayer about FAITHFULNESS

When I want to share God's faithfulness

HEAVENLY FATHER,

I'm grateful for the opportunity to share your faithfulness with the next generation. I want to leave a rich heritage by building awareness of your faithful love in the minds of the children who are a part of my life. Lord, may my words and actions combine to sing a duet of faithfulness to you, and may my life give those who come behind me an example to treasure throughout their lifetimes. That's the best legacy I can leave.

Each generation tells of your faithfulness to the next.
ISAIAH 38:19

DAY 85

A prayer about the HOLY SPIRIT
When I ponder how the Holy Spirit helps me

HEAVENLY FATHER,

You have given me the precious gift of the Holy Spirit—your very presence within me! Your Spirit helps me to understand your deep truths and to discover the wonders of your character. The Holy Spirit also convicts me of my sin, pointing out the truth of what I am doing compared to what I should be doing. By myself I'm weak, but I have you in me, showing me right from wrong, good from bad, and your way from the way of the world. I'm amazed that you care enough to give me one-on-one instruction and counsel on how to live a life that pleases you. Thank you, Lord, for this wonderful gift. May my heart always be responsive to the Spirit's teaching and leading so that this gift may never go to waste.

The Holy Spirit produces this kind of fruit in our lives: love, joy, peace, patience, kindness, goodness, faithfulness, gentleness, and self-control. There is no law against these things! Those who belong to Christ Jesus have nailed the passions and desires of their sinful nature to his cross and crucified them there. Since we are living by the Spirit, let us follow the Spirit's leading in every part of our lives.

GALATIANS 5:22-25

A prayer about HURTING OTHERS
When I have hurt someone

LORD,

I confess that I have hurt others—sometimes accidentally and sometimes intentionally. I have acted without regard for those around me, trying to get my own way. I have used my words to retaliate when others have hurt me first. I have acted in cold and hateful ways toward others, often just because my pride was injured. And I have neglected to offer compassion or help, even when I could see the needs before me. Forgive me, Lord. I am ashamed of my own pettiness and lack of compassion. You are full of unconditional love, and that can never be compatible with intentionally hurting others. I want to be like you. Please wash me clean and fill me with your love for those around me so that I may treat them the way I should.

All of you should be of one mind. Sympathize with each other. Love each other as brothers and sisters. Be tender-hearted, and keep a humble attitude. Don't repay evil for evil. Don't retaliate with insults when people insult you. Instead, pay them back with a blessing. That is what God has called you to do, and he will bless you for it.

1 PETER 3:8-9

DAY 87

✓ A prayer about LIMITATIONS
When I wonder how God could use me

LORD GOD,
I feel so weak and limited, and I wonder what I can possibly do for your Kingdom. But when I start to question my usefulness to you, I am reminded of the many times in the Bible when you took doubting, unqualified people and used them greatly. Gideon said he was "the least" of his family, but you called him a mighty hero! He wasn't yet a hero, but with your help and direction, he became one. I look at my limitations, but you see my potential. I see my weakness, but you see the woman you intended me to be—the woman you created me to be. O Father, help me learn to see life from your perspective. You, almighty God of the universe, look at me for what I can become with your help rather than for what I am! Thank you for encouraging me this way. May I never hide from your call, thinking I am unqualified. Instead, may I respond with courage, knowing that you will never call me to a task without fully equipping me to do it. You will bring out the best in me.

All glory to God, who is able, through his mighty power at work within us, to accomplish infinitely more than we might ask or think. EPHESIANS 3:20

A prayer about RELEVANCE
When I wonder if the Bible is relevant today

HEAVENLY FATHER,
Sometimes I wonder how the Bible can still be relevant so many years after it was written. But when I look at how it has stood the test of time, I am amazed. Recovered manuscripts show that the text has not changed over centuries. Archaeological findings confirm many of the described events. The Bible has been faithfully preserved because it contains your very words. You have promised not to let them disappear from the earth or allow them to be altered by human hands. Your words apply to all generations, cultures, and peoples, yet they speak to me individually as well! May I always approach your Word with reverence, believing that it is living and active, offering wisdom for my life and a picture of you, my Creator. Soften my heart as I read Scripture, Lord, so that my life may be changed by your unchanging words.

[The LORD *says,] "The rain and snow come down from the heavens and stay on the ground to water the earth. They cause the grain to grow, producing seed for the farmer and bread for the hungry. It is the same with my word. I send it out, and it always produces fruit. It will accomplish all I want it to, and it will prosper everywhere I send it."*
ISAIAH 55:10-11

A prayer about RESPECT
When I'm seeking respect from others

HEAVENLY FATHER,

I want others to respect me, but I may be trying to gain respect in the wrong way. The world encourages me to look beautiful at all costs, to act with confidence when I'm scared, to speak with irreverence, and to live by what's best for *me*. But that's a self-centered and unearned way to try to grab respect. Ultimately, living like that will only embarrass me in the eyes of my peers. Your Word tells me that the best way to get respect is to live according to your values. Teach me that when I consistently practice kindness, live with integrity, and am motivated by a deep love of others, I will reflect your character. And the more I exude your love to others, the more I will become the kind of woman who truly earns respect. Lord, please give me the integrity and patience to earn respect the right way—through living to please you.

Even the Son of Man came not to be served but to serve others and to give his life as a ransom for many.
MARK 10:45

DAY 90 *Prayerful Moment*

A prayer about EXPERIENCING GOD
When I want to live in contact with God

HEAVENLY FATHER,
I don't want to go through the motions of faith. I want to genuinely be in contact with you! Grant me a pure, soft heart that will be ready to experience your work in me. Thank you for your Holy Spirit, who instructs me and inspires me to respond with obedience. Give me the insight to recognize your Spirit encouraging me, empowering me, and guiding me in your ways.

God blesses those whose hearts are pure, for they will see God.
MATTHEW 5:8

DAY 91 *Prayerful Moment*

A prayer about NEEDING GOD
When I need to seek the Lord

HEAVENLY FATHER,
I need you every hour. Sometimes I don't notice my need, but today it's heavy upon me. May I respond by seeking you wholeheartedly. Your Word tells me that when I look for you, I will find you. O Lord, may I find a quiet place in which to escape from this busy world and listen for your voice. Speak to me, that I may be refreshed and come forth ready again to follow you.

When you pray, go away by yourself, shut the door behind you, and pray to your Father in private. Then your Father, who sees everything, will reward you. MATTHEW 6:6

A prayer about SERVICE

When I wonder if God can use my limited experience

DEAR LORD,

When I feel out of my league and too inexperienced for the task ahead of me, I remember that you waste nothing. You use everything to further your purposes. After all, King David came to the throne with a résumé that included shepherding as his first job—but you used that background to prepare him to rule, not as a tyrant, but as a caring shepherd. Help me to remember that you can use me in whatever situation I find myself and that you will use my circumstances to prepare me for future service. I am a part of your plan! As I obey you, may you carry out your purposes through me. Use all my varied training and experience, God, to make me more fruitful for you.

[Jesus said,] "You didn't choose me. I chose you. I appointed you to go and produce lasting fruit, so that the Father will give you whatever you ask for, using my name."

JOHN 15:16

A prayer about LISTENING
When I'm not sure that God hears my prayers

FATHER,

Sometimes it feels as though my prayers are bouncing off the ceiling. I just don't see any response. Are you paying attention? Do you hear me? But when these doubts come from my lips, you plant another question in my mind: am I paying attention? I know from your Word and from my own life that you do answer prayer. You are loving and good, and it's in your nature to give good things to your people. But after a problem is resolved, it's easy for me to take the solution for granted and fail to give you the credit. Sometimes I don't even notice that you answered! O Lord, when I pray, may I be alert and watch for your response, even if it isn't what I expected. Help me respond with gratitude, thanking you for hearing me. I trust in your goodness, and I know that no matter what your answer is, it's the right answer.

Devote yourselves to prayer with an alert mind and a thankful heart. COLOSSIANS 4:2

A prayer about PERSECUTION

When I face scorn or mockery because of my faith

LORD JESUS,

Compared to people in other places in the world, I know I don't experience much persecution for following you. After all, I am free to worship you without fear of losing my job or being arrested. Yet sometimes I am scorned, mocked, or ignored by others because of my faith. That's hard for me to deal with. Please remind me that it's during these hard times that my character is being stretched and my real self is being exposed. Help me to endure whatever persecution comes my way so that all will see that my trust in you is real. Your Word is full of people who hung on to their faith in you no matter what happened. They never stopped trusting you even though they were mocked, persecuted, and in some cases killed. Empower me, Lord, to live boldly for you, no matter what the opposition. May my life have an impact for eternity.

Be on guard. Stand firm in the faith. Be courageous. Be strong. 1 CORINTHIANS 16:13

A prayer about the BIBLE
When I forget why I should study God's Word

ALMIGHTY GOD,

I praise you that your Word is a living document, relevant for all people in all times and places. When I read it, you communicate with me. Reading the Bible keeps me in your presence—with you, the one who created me for a purpose, who knows me best, and who can guide me along the best pathway for my life. What a blessing! Soften my heart. Make me receptive to the words recorded in your book so that I will desire to read it daily and will begin to gain comfort, joy, insight, wisdom, knowledge, and the keys to living. I want to experience daily divine moments with you by reading your Word.

The instructions of the LORD are perfect, reviving the soul. The decrees of the LORD are trustworthy, making wise the simple. The commandments of the LORD are right, bringing joy to the heart. The commands of the LORD are clear, giving insight for living. PSALM 19:7-8

DAY 96

A prayer about STUBBORNNESS
When my stubborn attitude is affecting my life

FATHER,

I need you to break through my stubbornness. Sometimes I am so set on my ideas that I don't want to admit that your plan for my life might actually be better. Other times I get stuck in my refusal to believe that you really care or that you could even make a difference in my situation. I end up in a prison of my own stubbornness, not trusting you or even praying to you, and I can't get out. Only you can change my heart. Help me to humble myself, Lord—to admit that you know the better path. Forgive me for my hardheaded determination to go my own way. Teach me to acknowledge your wisdom, your love, and your power, even when I can't see them. Help me to give up my need to be right, and soften my heart toward you and others. May I never turn away.

Be careful then, dear brothers and sisters. Make sure that your own hearts are not evil and unbelieving, turning you away from the living God. You must warn each other every day, while it is still "today," so that none of you will be deceived by sin and hardened against God. For if we are faithful to the end, trusting God just as firmly as when we first believed, we will share in all that belongs to Christ.

HEBREWS 3:12-14

DAY 97 *Prayerful Moment*

A prayer about FORGIVENESS
When I need to forgive someone

MERCIFUL GOD,
I am struggling to forgive someone. I know that sometimes I must *decide* to forgive before the feelings of mercy will come. Help me always to remember that when I choose to forgive someone who has wronged me, I will be freed from the bitterness and resentment that can saturate my soul. As I release the hurt, you will heal me. May I not waste another moment, but forgive by your grace so that I can move past my hurt into the future you have for me.

Forgive us our sins, as we have forgiven those who sin against us. MATTHEW 6:12

DAY 98 *Prayerful Moment*

A prayer about INITIATIVE
When I recognize God's initiative in my life

LORD,
I thank you that you took the initiative to have a relationship with me. You changed my heart so that I would desire you, and you softened my heart so I could see my own sin and my need of you. Thank you that when you convict me of wrongdoing, you don't abandon me. You guide me back to the right path. You are faithful to stay with me, molding me into the woman you created me to be.

God showed his great love for us by sending Christ to die for us while we were still sinners. ROMANS 5:8

A prayer about PERSPECTIVE
When I wonder if there's a pattern to my life

DEAR LORD,

From my human perspective, the world and events in my own life often seem to be random and unpredictable. But your Word clearly states that you are still in control and that people's sinful ways do not ruin your sovereign plans. You can use even someone's poor choices to fulfill your bigger plan—just as the unjust treatment Joseph suffered at the hands of his brothers fulfilled your plan to save Jacob's descendants from famine and bring them to Egypt. I have faith in your eternal, comprehensive plan, and I believe that someday I will be able to see that you have made my life a beautiful tapestry. Right now I can see only sections of the back, with all of its knots and loose ends. But I trust that someday in heaven I will see the front in its entirety—the picture of world history and my own life from your perspective. How amazing that will be! So today give me the grace to interpret unexpected and even unwelcome circumstances as part of your grand plan. When I do, I know I'll be able to embrace both the good and the bad, knowing that you are weaving a beautiful picture with my life.

The LORD will work out his plans for my life.
PSALM 138:8

DAY 100

A prayer about UNCONDITIONAL LOVE
When I want to love unconditionally

FATHER,

I'm so limited in my expression of love to those around me. When I am angry or feel hurt, my tendency is to withdraw from the one who hurt me. When my family or my friends disappoint me, I don't feel kindness toward them. But your Word makes clear that I am called to love. Help me to follow your perfect example of loving unconditionally. Teach me that agape love is more about action than feeling—doing the right thing even when I don't feel like it. Grant me the self-discipline to act with kindness even to those who may be undeserving; remind me that you love me even when I don't deserve it. I know that loving unconditionally doesn't mean having no boundaries; after all, the Old Testament shows that you loved the Israelites with your whole heart yet still allowed them to suffer consequences for their idolatry. But you loved them, and me, just the same.

May you have the power to understand, as all God's people should, how wide, how long, how high, and how deep his love is. May you experience the love of Christ, though it is too great to understand fully. Then you will be made complete with all the fullness of life and power that comes from God.
EPHESIANS 3:18-19

DAY 101

A prayer about HELP

When I realize I can't do everything by myself

HEAVENLY FATHER,

I'm so aware of my limitations, weaknesses, lack of skill, and feelings of inadequacy. Sometimes I just don't know what to do or how to do it. I've hit a crisis now, and I can't handle it by myself—I need your help. Thank you for creating me to be in relationship with you and with other people. You don't expect me to be self-sufficient and do everything alone; you have wired me both to receive help and to give it to others. Lord, I need help in so many areas—to get work done, to restore a relationship, to develop my skills, to think through a problem, to say "I'm sorry" when my heart is hard. You are the ultimate helper, for you are wise, strong, and infinitely loving. May I stop trying to do everything by myself and cultivate the habit of seeking help from you and from others. In turn, may I be willing to lend a hand to those around me who are in need.

The LORD is my strength and shield. I trust him with all my heart. He helps me, and my heart is filled with joy.

PSALM 28:7

A prayer about MENTORING

When I want to encourage godliness in a younger generation

HEAVENLY FATHER,

You have sent the Holy Spirit as my spiritual mentor. Through him, you help me to build a relationship with you, and you guide me into wisdom, maturity, and understanding. I am so thankful for this gift of mentoring, and I would love to use it to help others. If you have someone for me to mentor, please guide me to the right person. May I commit to building a relationship with another woman where I can share wisdom, life experience, and support to help her learn and grow. I'm not perfect, Lord, but that's not what you ask of me. All you ask is that I focus on your faithfulness and share that with another—for your glory.

Teach the older women to live in a way that honors God. They must not slander others or be heavy drinkers. Instead, they should teach others what is good. These older women must train the younger women to love their husbands and their children, to live wisely and be pure, to work in their homes, to do good, and to be submissive to their husbands. Then they will not bring shame on the word of God.

TITUS 2:3-5

A prayer about WORK

When I wonder how I can glorify God whether I work or stay at home

HEAVENLY FATHER,

Being a woman is challenging, whether or not I work outside the home. Sometimes the tasks seem unending and thankless, and I grow weary. Help me to remember that my work is anchored in your character. You are a God of excellence and commitment, so I want to exhibit those same qualities in whatever job you've called me to. Even if no one else sees what I do, I want to work to the best of my ability, demonstrating creativity, responsibility, and loving care. I'm so thankful for the blessing of my family, and I know that you have placed me here for this stage of my life. Whether I'm at work or at home, help me to take the opportunity to demonstrate your standard of excellence and commitment to those around me. May my family see and be encouraged by my efforts to support them and glorify you.

Whatever you do or say, do it as a representative of the Lord Jesus, giving thanks through him to God the Father.

COLOSSIANS 3:17

DAY 104 *Prayerful Moment*

✓ A prayer about PEACE
When I need God's peace

LORD,
When my life starts to spin out of control, I know that prayer is my gateway to peace. I unburden my soul to you, knowing that you are the only one who can handle my problems. Your peace protects me from assaults of anxiety. O Lord, teach me that when I'm focused on my own problems, they will control me. Instead, may I turn my eyes toward you. When I seek you first, I will be able to experience peace despite my circumstances.

You will keep in perfect peace all who trust in you, all whose thoughts are fixed on you! ISAIAH 26:3

✓ DAY 105 *Prayerful Moment*

A prayer about WOMEN
When I thank God for valuing women

LORD JESUS,
When I read the Gospel accounts, I am amazed that you ministered to women in all levels of society. Most leaders of that day treated women as second-class citizens, but you spoke with them directly, healed them, and allowed them to travel with you and your disciples. Lord, I thank you that you love and value women. You never view me as second best, and you have a purpose for my life.

In those days I will pour out my Spirit even on servants—men and women alike. JOEL 2:29

DAY 106

✓ A prayer about GOD'S HAND
When I want to see God working

DEAR LORD,

I know that you work in different ways in my life. Sometimes you demonstrate your power through visible signs; at other times your power is much more subtle, working in my heart as I seek you. Sometimes you work through events in my life, and sometimes you are a still, quiet voice in my mind. Help me to be diligent in trusting you and always expectant about how you want to work your will through me. I know that often it's not until I look back on a chapter of my life that I can see your fingerprints. I'm thankful that though your way of working in me changes, *you* never change. Your love, your law, and your promises are constant. May I always trust you and watch for the ways you work. Give me eyes to see the divine moments when your hand is on me.

God works in different ways, but it is the same God who does the work in all of us. 1 CORINTHIANS 12:6

DAY 107

A prayer about WORSHIP
When I wonder why it's difficult to worship

O LORD,

You are worthy of all my worship—my extravagant devotion. I want to acknowledge your power and glory; I want to experience your presence through the Holy Spirit. Yet sometimes it is difficult for me to humble myself in worship. In so much of my life I'm used to being in charge, but genuine worship calls me to submit myself to you. I'm used to glossing over my shortcomings, but true worship calls me to recognize and confess my sinfulness. Teach me, Lord, that only through humble praise and adoration will I begin to recognize who you are, and who I am in comparison. May my heart be filled with gratitude when I realize how you have lifted me up through your grace and forgiveness. Whenever I see your wisdom, power, direction, care, and love in my life, may I respond with praise. Then worship will become second nature to me.

Oh, how great are God's riches and wisdom and knowledge! How impossible it is for us to understand his decisions and his ways! For who can know the LORD's thoughts? Who knows enough to give him advice? And who has given him so much that he needs to pay it back? For everything comes from him and exists by his power and is intended for his glory. All glory to him forever! Amen. ROMANS 11:33-36

A prayer about RENEWAL
When I need to start over

LORD,
I disappoint myself so often. I have such high hopes and good intentions, but inevitably I become weary and burned out. Sometimes the cause is a consequence of my bad choices or sinful actions. Other times it's the burden of everyday living—the simple busyness of work, family, and responsibilities. The messiness of life can leave me feeling exhausted not only physically but in my very soul. I sometimes wish I could just start over. I need your renewal in my life! I'm thankful that you have compassion on me. When my heart is ready for change, you can begin to work. You will restore me, refresh my soul, revive my life, and give me a new beginning. Thank you, Lord!

Purify me from my sins, and I will be clean; wash me, and I will be whiter than snow. Oh, give me back my joy again; you have broken me—now let me rejoice. Don't keep looking at my sins. Remove the stain of my guilt. Create in me a clean heart, O God. Renew a loyal spirit within me. Do not banish me from your presence, and don't take your Holy Spirit from me. Restore to me the joy of your salvation, and make me willing to obey you. PSALM 51:7-12

DAY 109

✓ A prayer about JUDGING OTHERS
When I need to stop being critical

LORD GOD,

When I see a wrong attitude or behavior in people who are close to me, I can choose how I will react. All too often, I respond with judgment. I criticize or lecture without any intent to see them succeed or improve. In the process I hurt their feelings and may even drive them further away. But that's not your way. You call me to look at my own behavior before I offer an opinion about someone else's. That's the first step in learning to respond with an attitude of humility and love. Only with that mind-set will I be able to offer constructive criticism, in which my goal is to build relationships and help others become who you created them to be. Guard my thoughts and lips, keeping me from harsh judgment. Remind me always to let love be my guide.

Do not judge others, and you will not be judged. For you will be treated as you treat others. The standard you use in judging is the standard by which you will be judged. And why worry about a speck in your friend's eye when you have a log in your own? MATTHEW 7:1-3

A prayer about FASTING
When I consider fasting

LORD,

Fasting has not been a regular part of my life, but when I read the Bible I see that fasting has frequently been a part of worship. Jesus talked about it when he was on earth and assumed God's people would fast. I don't want to discount fasting, but I need your wisdom to discern how to incorporate it into my life. I can see that abstaining from food might help me to focus on you, even allowing me to have a sharper mind that's especially receptive to what you have to say. Teach me how fasting can improve my communication with you by eliminating my usual routine and freeing me to spend more time with you. As I consider fasting, Lord, I ask that you would use it to break through the barriers that keep me from giving myself to you wholeheartedly. Use this discipline to draw me to yourself, for your glory.

[Jesus said,] "When you fast, don't make it obvious, as the hypocrites do, for they try to look miserable and disheveled so people will admire them for their fasting. I tell you the truth, that is the only reward they will ever get. But when you fast, comb your hair and wash your face. Then no one will notice that you are fasting, except your Father, who knows what you do in private. And your Father, who sees everything, will reward you." MATTHEW 6:16-18

DAY 111 *Prayerful Moment*

✓ **A prayer about REPENTANCE**
When I need to turn away from my sin

FATHER GOD,
I realize that I've been going the wrong way in life. I confess my sin to you and ask you to forgive me. I want to repent—to change my direction. I need your help to move away from my sinful habits and move toward you. Only you can change me so I can experience your fullest blessings, both now and for eternity. May my heart be soft and ready to accept your loving guidance so I will be moving in the right direction.

[The Lord says,] "Come back to me, and I will heal your wayward hearts." JEREMIAH 3:22

✓
DAY 112 *Prayerful Moment*

A prayer about SEEKING GOD
When God seems to be hiding from me

LORD,
Sometimes you seem so far away. Yet your Word assures me that you want me to know you, and you reveal yourself in many ways—through your creation, through your Word, and even directly in my heart. May I have the courage to seek you, even when I know that finding you means I will be radically changed. You have promised that I will find you, the only one worth seeking, the only one that satisfies.

My heart has heard you say, "Come and talk with me." And my heart responds, "LORD, I am coming." PSALM 27:8

DAY 113

✓ A prayer about INVITATION

When I sense Jesus calling me to follow him

LORD JESUS,

When you invited Peter and Andrew to follow you, they responded. They left their nets—their very livelihood, since they were fishermen—and followed you. Their lives were never the same! They observed miracles; witnessed your resurrection; and, with the help of your transforming Holy Spirit, became pillars of the early church. You invite me to follow you too, and that invitation requires a decision: will I come into the adventure that awaits, or will I remain safe and comfortable where I am? My flesh wants to stay where things are predictable, but my heart hears your call. May I resist the pull of the familiar, leave the things I cling to for security, and follow you without turning back. I don't know what adventures await, but I trust you. I know I'll never regret it because the treasure I gain from following you will last forever.

Jesus called out to them, "Come, follow me, and I will show you how to fish for people!" And they left their nets at once and followed him. MATTHEW 4:19-20

✓ A prayer about REWARDS
When God rewards me for serving him

LORD,
You ask me to serve you freely, out of love—and I do! Yet your Word says that you reward those who serve you faithfully. Sometimes these rewards are tangible, material things, but not always. May I be aware of the times when following you has its own reward, such as when my obedience protects me from evil, leads me on the right paths to find more of your blessings, or directs me into service that will please you and help others. These are wonderful rewards. I'm also filled with gratitude when I consider the spiritual prosperity you promise: the gifts of salvation and eternal life; the blessings of a relationship with you; the treasure of your Word; and the wonderful character traits of godliness, truth, wisdom, and a good reputation. I thank you for these lasting, priceless rewards you shower on me when I follow you.

There truly is a reward for those who live for God; surely there is a God who judges justly here on earth.
PSALM 58:11

✓ A prayer about ANGER
When I'm struggling with my anger

HOLY GOD,

Why do I get so angry? Sometimes it's a reaction to my pride being hurt. When I'm confronted, rejected, ignored, or don't get my way, I use anger as a defense mechanism to protect my ego. I get upset when someone confronts me about my sinful actions because I don't want to admit I've done something wrong—and I don't want anyone else to know it either. O Lord, when anger begins to well up inside me, teach me to stop before it gets out of control. When my reaction is really about my own pride, may I recognize that and confess it. Then I know my anger will melt away, leaving room for a more thoughtful, humble response. Guard my tongue so that my angry words will not hurt others. May I learn to follow your example of being slow to become angry.

The LORD is compassionate and merciful, slow to get angry and filled with unfailing love. He will not constantly accuse us, nor remain angry forever. PSALM 103:8-9

A prayer about SELF-SACRIFICE
When I need to put aside my self-interests

LORD JESUS,

You have called me to put others before myself. I know that's the best path, but some days it goes against my every desire! Left to myself, too often I will seek my own good over the good of others. Whether it's as minor as wanting to choose the restaurant when we go out or as major as ignoring a family member's significant need, it's easy to serve my own self-interests. But when I remember your example, I am rebuked. You put aside your own divine nature and let yourself be humbled, even to the point of death on the cross—all because you put others' well-being above your own. May I learn from your example. Transform my heart and make me willing to put aside my own needs for the good of others. I pray that when I do that, others will see your love shining through me.

Don't be selfish; don't try to impress others. Be humble, thinking of others as better than yourselves. Don't look out only for your own interests, but take an interest in others, too.
PHILIPPIANS 2:3-4

DAY 117

A prayer about TESTING
When my faith is being tested

LORD,

Just as students are tested regularly to see if they have understood and retained what they have been taught, so also I sometimes face testing. My character and spiritual commitments are tested by the fires of hardship, persecution, or suffering. Your Word, in James 1:13, tells me that you will not tempt me to sin, but you do use testing to purify me and move me toward maturity and growth. I resist this, Lord, but help me to see it as an opportunity to develop a more committed faith—because as I do, I will also become a wiser and more committed woman. Strengthen my resolve so that I can accomplish all you want me to. Whenever I feel as if my faith is being tested, give me the grace to see you moving in my life to strengthen my relationship with you.

Dear brothers and sisters, when troubles come your way, consider it an opportunity for great joy. For you know that when your faith is tested, your endurance has a chance to grow. So let it grow, for when your endurance is fully developed, you will be perfect and complete, needing nothing.

JAMES 1:2-4

DAY 118 *Prayerful Moment*

✓ A prayer about OBEDIENCE
When I need to obey God

LORD GOD,
Sometimes I chafe against the idea of obedience. I want to do things my way! But as I study your Word, I realize that your commandments are not burdensome obligations but pathways to a joyful, meaningful, and satisfying life. You call me to obedience because you are committed to my well-being. You created life, so you know the best way to live. Teach me to obey your commands and trust your direction.

God is working in you, giving you the desire and the power to do what pleases him. PHILIPPIANS 2:13

✓ DAY 119 *Prayerful Moment*

A prayer about JOY
When I want to experience great joy

LORD GOD,
I want to know the joy that comes from walking with you. I want joy that's more than happiness, that's like a strong current running deep beneath the sometimes stormy surface of my feelings. My soul longs for the joy that comes from knowing I am held by you, the eternal God, and from knowing you accept me for who I am and want me with you in eternity. Open my heart to experience this joy, Lord. I thank you for being a God of joy.

Always be full of joy in the Lord. I say it again—rejoice!
PHILIPPIANS 4:4

DAY 120

A prayer about REGRETS
When I'm haunted by regret

LOVING GOD,

I am weighed down by guilt and regret over my past. Guilt is my spiritual response to sin, and regret is the sorrow I feel over the consequences of my decisions. I have sought your forgiveness for my sins, and you have promised to remove my guilt. When I came to faith in Jesus, you forgave all my sins! I praise you that you choose not to remember my past but to give me a fresh start. This is a wonderful truth, even though I still have to live with the consequences of my sin. Help me deal with my regrets so that I may move on without this heavy load. Sorrow over my past choices often consumes my thoughts and keeps me from serving you. Please free me! Let me truly grasp the power of your forgiveness, and in doing so, may I then turn my regrets into a resolve to make better choices in the future. I can't do this by myself, Lord. I rest in your power.

Oh, what joy for those whose disobedience is forgiven, whose sin is put out of sight! Yes, what joy for those whose record the L*ORD has cleared of guilt, whose lives are lived in complete honesty!* PSALM 32:1-2

DAY 121

A prayer about SHARING

When I want to become more generous

HEAVENLY FATHER,

I've been taught to share since early childhood, yet I still find it difficult to give of my resources or of myself. At the very core of my sinful human nature is a desire to get, not give; to accumulate, not relinquish; to look out for myself, not for others. Yet your Word calls me to share many things—my resources, my faith, my love, my time, my talents, my money. You ask me to share because you have shared so generously with me. May I respond in gratitude, Lord, sharing with others as an expression of my love for you. I know that as I share my gifts and resources, I will be passing on your blessings to others. The added benefit is that many things are more enjoyable when I share them with others. Help me to discover that the benefits of giving generously are far greater than the temporary satisfaction of receiving.

May you be filled with joy, always thanking the Father. He has enabled you to share in the inheritance that belongs to his people, who live in the light. COLOSSIANS 1:11-12

DAY 122

A prayer about SPIRITUAL WARFARE
When I recognize that spiritual enemies are real

ALMIGHTY GOD,

I often get so caught up in what I can see that I forget about the spiritual enemies I can't see. But I know they are there. Your Word clearly teaches that humans are involved in a spiritual battle, and my faith in you puts me right in the middle of it. Help me to recognize that and protect myself with your armor so I will not be overwhelmed. I need your power to stand strong, to resist temptation, and to help me face the unseen enemy. Please protect me, God. Most of all, give me the peace that comes from knowing that you have already won the battle over death and evil! You are the ultimate victor over Satan, and you have the power to save me.

We are not fighting against flesh-and-blood enemies, but against evil rulers and authorities of the unseen world, against mighty powers in this dark world, and against evil spirits in the heavenly places. Therefore, put on every piece of God's armor so you will be able to resist the enemy in the time of evil. Then after the battle you will still be standing firm. EPHESIANS 6:12-13

A prayer about INTERCESSION

When I contemplate the difference that intercessory prayer makes

LOVING FATHER,

Some of the people I care about are struggling, and I get discouraged when I think there is nothing I can do to help. But you remind me that the most important thing I can do is pray. Your Word is full of stories that illustrate the miraculous power that comes when your people cry out to you. Abraham interceded effectively for an entire city, and you sent an angel to rescue the apostle Peter from prison as believers were holding an all-night prayer meeting. May I never doubt that you do hear and answer prayer, although not always in the way or the timing I would choose. I may not completely understand it, but I have faith that praying for others opens up a channel for your love and power. It can create a deep bond between people as well; when I pray for someone else, my heart is softened toward that person and my compassion increases. Thank you for the powerful tool of prayer, Lord. May I never doubt its effectiveness, and may I never take it for granted.

The earnest prayer of a righteous person has great power and produces wonderful results. JAMES 5:16

A prayer about FLEXIBILITY
When I'm struggling to be available to God

FATHER GOD,

I like to know what's ahead. I plan out my days, my weeks, and sometimes even my years. I enjoy this kind of planning, yet I realize that I'm missing some opportunities because I lack flexibility. Your timing does not always match mine, and I want to allow room in my life to change my plans so they mesh with yours. I want to be available to you, Lord. Show me how to be flexible so that I can avoid anything that might take my focus off you. I want to be able to devote myself to you completely whenever you call. May I be eager to go where you call me and serve where you place me, even if it means changing my wants. That's a form of taking up my cross—putting to death my own selfish desires—and following you. Guard me from rigidness, and prepare me for wonderful surprise moments as you guide me through life.

[Jesus said,] "If any of you wants to be my follower, you must turn from your selfish ways, take up your cross, and follow me. If you try to hang on to your life, you will lose it. But if you give up your life for my sake and for the sake of the Good News, you will save it." MARK 8:34-35

DAY 125 *Prayerful Moment*

✓ A prayer about the HEART
When I want to seek God

LOVING FATHER,
I want you to be the center of my life. When you are, my relationship with you is my highest priority. I long to spend time in prayer and reading your Word. My thoughts often turn to you, and I want to please you and obey you. O Father, may I always put you first. Please transform my heart into one that treasures you above all.

Wherever your treasure is, there the desires of your heart will also be. LUKE 12:34

✓ DAY 126 *Prayerful Moment*

A prayer about MEMORIES
When I need to overcome memories that are keeping me in the past

HEAVENLY FATHER,
I'm still holding on to old memories of my life. But I realize that it's virtually impossible for me to obey you if I'm still looking backward. I need your help so I don't dwell on these memories and, instead, experience the better life you offer. Empower me to fix my eyes on heaven and look forward to everything you have prepared for me as your child.

We don't look at the troubles we can see now; rather, we fix our gaze on things that cannot be seen.
2 CORINTHIANS 4:18

A prayer about REST

When I feel called to times of quiet

HEAVENLY FATHER,

When I feel off or dissatisfied, I know I need to renew my fellowship with you. I pray for the self-discipline to find time to be quiet before you. Restore me. I know that when I connect with you, I tap into your strength, and that is what I need right now. I am weak; I have worn myself out with constant activity in my attempts to be productive. But now I see that I need to slow down in order to speed up. Even Jesus, amid his busy ministry, saw the importance of finding time for rest and quiet reflection. As I follow his example, help me to stop awhile to let my body, mind, and spirit recover. Reset my purpose so that I can be more energized and productive when I'm ready to get back to the work at hand. Show me how to find the balance between work and rest, investment in people and quiet time for restoration.

Jesus said, "Let's go off by ourselves to a quiet place and rest awhile." He said this because there were so many people coming and going that Jesus and his apostles didn't even have time to eat. So they left by boat for a quiet place.

MARK 6:31-32

√ ## A prayer about KINDNESS
When I contemplate God's kindness to me

LORD GOD,
Your abundant kindness is evident all around me. You show it by inviting me into an eternal relationship with you, loving me unconditionally, being patient when I sin, and forgiving me. Giving me time to turn from my sins and choose your way of life shows your kind heart. And your kindness is evident when you meet my physical and spiritual needs: you send the rain, sun, and harvests to care for me physically; you also send spiritual refreshment to care for my soul. Your Word says that you are love—and love is kind. Thank you for showering your kindness on me. May I in turn reflect your character by showering kindness on others.

The LORD is merciful and compassionate, slow to get angry and filled with unfailing love. The LORD is good to everyone. He showers compassion on all his creation. . . . The LORD is righteous in everything he does; he is filled with kindness. PSALM 145:8-9, 17

✓ A prayer about MOTIVATION
When I need motivation in my spiritual life

FATHER,

When I've lost my enthusiasm in my relationship with you, it's often because my faith has become shallow. If my trust in you lacks depth, there's no place for the seeds of your Word to grow, no way for them to take root. Then the hot sun of persecution or problems causes my excitement and my sense of purpose to wither. O Lord, may I have the self-discipline to read your Word and spend time in prayer, strengthening my relationship with you. I want to be deeply rooted in you, thriving under your care. As I do that, I know my enthusiasm for my tasks will increase. The joy and gratitude I feel because of you will be the best motivation to go ever deeper.

The seed on the rocky soil represents those who hear the message and immediately receive it with joy. But since they don't have deep roots, they don't last long. They fall away as soon as they have problems or are persecuted for believing God's word. . . . The seed that fell on good soil represents those who truly hear and understand God's word and produce a harvest of thirty, sixty, or even a hundred times as much as had been planted! MATTHEW 13:20-21, 23

A prayer about FUN

When I wonder whether God values celebration

LORD GOD,

I'm amazed when I read through the Old Testament and see the number of feasts and festivals you instituted for the Israelites. Some of those had serious religious meanings, but they also were times of immense celebration for your people. You took pleasure in their joy. Thank you that you want me to laugh and enjoy life! The fun I have on earth is just a small taste of the joy awaiting me in heaven. When I experience joy, fun, and celebration the way you intended—in balance with work and not conflicting with the moral codes you have given in your Word—my spirits are lifted. I can see more clearly the beauty and richness of life. Thank you, God, for blessing me with a taste of eternity.

For everything there is a season, a time for every activity under heaven. . . . A time to cry and a time to laugh. A time to grieve and a time to dance. ECCLESIASTES 3:1, 4

DAY 131

A prayer about FORGIVENESS

When I need to be reassured of God's forgiveness

MERCIFUL FATHER,

I have made a mess of things today. I confess my sin, and I need your forgiveness—again. It seems I struggle with this sin over and over, and I worry that I'm running out of chances with you. But when I remember the stories from the Old Testament, I'm reassured. The Israelites turned away from you to idols time and again, yet you kept calling them back. Every time, if they were truly repentant, you extended love and forgiveness, because you wanted a relationship with them. You wanted to be their God, and you set plans in place to bless them. They still suffered the natural consequences of their sin, and even though I can expect that in my life, too, I praise you for your patient and repeated forgiveness! You are my God.

If my people who are called by my name will humble themselves and pray and seek my face and turn from their wicked ways, I will hear from heaven and will forgive their sins and restore their land. 2 CHRONICLES 7:14

DAY 132 *Prayerful Moment*

✓ **A prayer about the FUTURE**
When I worry about the future

FATHER GOD,
I'm feeling insecure about the future, and that makes it easy to doubt your care for me. I'm tempted to think that you are not paying attention to me. Forgive me for doubting you, Lord. I know that you are my loving creator. You *are* love. How could you hold anything back? I cling to this hope as I look toward the future.

"I know the plans I have for you," says the LORD. "They are plans for good and not for disaster, to give you a future and a hope." JEREMIAH 29:11

✓ DAY 133 *Prayerful Moment*

A prayer about DIVERSITY
When I ponder the diverse body of Christ

HEAVENLY FATHER,
You designed me to contribute to the body of Christ, the church. The human body is made up of separate and different parts, yet all parts work together to sustain life. It's the same with your church. In your wisdom you have created a unique role for each believer. You're showing me that our diversity can enhance harmony. Teach me to be faithful in my part; may it help sustain the body of Christ and allow it to flourish.

All of you together are Christ's body, and each of you is a part of it. 1 CORINTHIANS 12:27

A prayer about VICTORY
When I want to experience victory

VICTORIOUS GOD,

With your help, the Israelites experienced victory after victory as they marched toward the Promised Land. My greatest victory, which was won by Christ, was when I received your wonderful gift of salvation. Yet daily I still need victory over the strongholds of sin that threaten my ability to live effectively for you and be a victorious example to others. Your Word tells me that if I want to experience victory in the Christian life, I must be willing to commit myself to vigorous spiritual training and preparation. Help me to make that my goal. May I pray without ceasing. May I consistently read your Word and obey it. O Lord, I want to make you my top priority. I know that when I put you first, I will conquer my fears. You will give me victory over Satan's tactics, which seek to derail my relationship with you and with those I love. You alone can cause me to be victorious over sin, and I rest in your power.

You are my hiding place; you protect me from trouble. You surround me with songs of victory. PSALM 32:7

A prayer about ACCEPTANCE
When I wonder if I'm acceptable to God

LOVING GOD,
Sometimes I wonder why you would want me as your follower. What do I have to offer you? Why would you seek after me? When I have these thoughts, I remember the truths in your Word. My very existence is proof of your faithful love for me! You created me in your own image so I could have a relationship with you. You chose me before the foundations of the world were laid. You made me and equipped me with abilities to use for your special purposes. You call me your child. Thank you, Lord. May I never forget these things, because when I do, I lose sight of who you really are, and I miss out on being useful to you.

God knew his people in advance, and he chose them to become like his Son, so that his Son would be the firstborn among many brothers and sisters. And having chosen them, he called them to come to him. And having called them, he gave them right standing with himself. And having given them right standing, he gave them his glory.
ROMANS 8:29-30

DAY 136

✓ A prayer about HABITS
When I need to break a bad habit

LORD GOD,

Voices in my culture tell me that I am a victim who has no power to resist the temptations around me. *It's not my fault*, I hear; *heredity, environment, or circumstances are to blame*. But this kind of thinking makes me only more vulnerable to my sinful desires. The wonderful truth is that you are more powerful than anything else that might seek to control me. Thank you, Lord. The fact is, I've let wrong desires sneak in and set up bad habits. Now I'm trying to fix those bad habits by taking back control of my thinking, but it's not working—I'm not able to on my own. Help me to realize that you alone can change me. Through your Holy Spirit within me, I have access to your transforming power. Unleash that in me! As I ask for your help and seek support from other believers, may you break the chains that hold me. Set me free from bad habits.

Do not let sin control the way you live; do not give in to sinful desires. Do not let any part of your body become an instrument of evil to serve sin. Instead, give yourselves completely to God, for you were dead, but now you have new life. So use your whole body as an instrument to do what is right for the glory of God. Sin is no longer your master, for you no longer live under the requirements of the law. Instead, you live under the freedom of God's grace.

ROMANS 6:12-14

A prayer about ENEMIES
When I wonder how I can love my enemies

LORD JESUS,
You taught that we are to love our enemies and to do good to those who curse us. But how do I do that when it goes against everything I feel? When I think of people who have hurt me or my loved ones, my wounded pride and my desire to protect my family stand in the way of forgiveness. Yet your Word, in Romans 5:10, tells me that *I* was once your enemy until you forgave me. How can I not follow your example? Teach me to see my enemies as you do—as people in need of grace and forgiveness. As I pray for people who have hurt me, please renew a sense of compassion in my heart. Work in me so that my response to my enemies might be full of your love and grace. Perhaps someone will see your forgiveness in me and will be moved to turn to you.

Love your enemies! Do good to them. Lend to them without expecting to be repaid. Then your reward from heaven will be very great, and you will truly be acting as children of the Most High, for he is kind to those who are unthankful and wicked. You must be compassionate, just as your Father is compassionate. LUKE 6:35-36

A prayer about NEGLECTING GOD
When I realize I'm neglecting God

LORD GOD,

I confess that I sometimes make excuses for why I can't serve you. Maybe it doesn't feel like the right time to start the practice of daily Bible study or to begin tithing. Or maybe I think I'm just too busy to stop a sinful habit or share the gospel with my non-Christian friends. But the reality is that it comes down to my priorities. If something is important enough to me, I will make time to do it. Please forgive me, Lord, for neglecting you and the things you ask of me. I'm making excuses, but really the problem is my stubborn heart and my fearful spirit. I want to make you my top priority—not just in my words but in my actions. As I do that, please open my eyes to see your active work and blessing in my life.

What good is it, dear brothers and sisters, if you say you have faith but don't show it by your actions? Can that kind of faith save anyone? JAMES 2:14

DAY 139 *Prayerful Moment*

✓ A prayer about GOD'S CALL
When I wonder what God has called me to

FATHER,
I want to answer your call for my life, but I'm not always sure what that is. As I'm studying your Word and waiting for clear direction, help me to develop the special abilities you have given me and begin to use them. As I do, Lord, please show me more specifically what you want me to pursue. May your calling fill my thoughts and energies, creating in me a longing to pursue it wholeheartedly.

God's gifts and his call can never be withdrawn.
ROMANS 11:29

DAY 140 *Prayerful Moment*

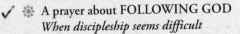

✓ A prayer about FOLLOWING GOD
When discipleship seems difficult

FATHER,
Following you is not easy. In fact, sometimes it seems that the more important a task is, the more obstacles I face. When you are leading me in a certain direction, give me the courage not to give up, even when the going gets tough. May I keep moving forward boldly with my eyes fixed on you. I know that you will strengthen my faith as I obey you.

Jesus said to his disciples, "If any of you wants to be my follower, you must turn from your selfish ways, take up your cross, and follow me." MATTHEW 16:24

A prayer about COMPARISONS
When I struggle with comparing myself to others

LORD,

So often I look at the women around me and wonder how I compare. Satan tries to convince me that my worth is based on how well I measure up in how I look, what I own, what I can do, or what people think about me. But that just leaves me feeling either inadequate and envious or full of pride. I don't want either of those extremes, Father. Teach me to determine my worth by accepting your love for me. In your eyes I am valued and loved—as is everyone else. I need to find that balance between humility over my sin and exultation at your lavish grace, which has no comparison. Thank you for all the gracious ways you show your love to me.

Pay careful attention to your own work, for then you will get the satisfaction of a job well done, and you won't need to compare yourself to anyone else. For we are each responsible for our own conduct. GALATIANS 6:4-5

✓ A prayer about COURAGE
When I am afraid

FATHER,
I am often afraid, and I wish you would remove the things that frighten me. But I know that's not how you work. The early church faced terrible persecution, yet they didn't pray for the threats to end but for the courage to face them. May I follow their example. Please give me the boldness to turn the things that threaten me into opportunities for spiritual growth and for declaring my faith. When I'm frightened by the enormity of my problems, may I see them as opportunities to recognize that you are by my side. After all, if you took away everything that frightens me, I would have no need for courage. Help me see beyond the immediate crisis and put my future in your hands. This is the safest place to be.

All the believers lifted their voices together in prayer. . . . "O Lord, hear their threats, and give us, your servants, great boldness in preaching your word. Stretch out your hand with healing power; may miraculous signs and wonders be done through the name of your holy servant Jesus." After this prayer, the meeting place shook, and they were all filled with the Holy Spirit. Then they preached the word of God with boldness. ACTS 4:24, 29-31

A prayer about TITHING
When I ponder how giving reflects God's heart

GENEROUS GOD,

You pour out more blessings on me than I could ever deserve. The gift of life, the gift of love, the gift of salvation, the gift of eternity in heaven—all these are priceless, and I am forever grateful for your generosity. You originated the concept of giving! And one of the great and unique promises you made in your Word is that the more I give, the more I receive—not necessarily in material possessions, but in spiritual and eternal rewards. Thank you for that promise, Lord. May I invest myself in you and your Kingdom and follow your example in giving generously.

"Bring all the tithes into the storehouse so there will be enough food in my Temple. If you do," says the L*ORD of Heaven's Armies, "I will open the windows of heaven for you. I will pour out a blessing so great you won't have enough room to take it in! Try it! Put me to the test!"* MALACHI 3:10

✓ A prayer about BOREDOM
When I'm struggling with apathy

FATHER GOD,

Today I feel bored. My life sometimes falls into a mindless routine of doing the same tedious things over and over, whether it's at my job, with my family, or around the house. I need a renewed sense of purpose. I know there is significant work I can do for your Kingdom, Lord. Please guide me to the right thing. I know that serving you will energize me and make me excited again about what I can do with my life. May I look for opportunities to help others, whether through volunteering in a local ministry, developing a new skill, or serving in a new way at church. That will give me something to look forward to each day. But even in the day-to-day routine, teach me to find meaning by doing my work for you. Even the most mundane task can please you when I do it with love and a servant's heart. When I search for things that help me feel your pleasure, I know I'll never be bored.

Let's not get tired of doing what is good. At just the right time we will reap a harvest of blessing if we don't give up.
GALATIANS 6:9

A prayer about EVIL

When I wonder why God allows evil in the world

LORD,

I can't go an hour without being aware that evil exists in the world—and sometimes its presence seems overwhelming. When I wonder why you allow it, I always come back to the same thing: Genuine love requires the freedom to choose. You wanted a loving relationship with me, so you gave me the freedom to choose your way or my way. Too often I choose my own way, and no one knows better than I do that my way leads to sin. I know this breaks your heart, Lord, and it breaks mine, too. Help me to realize that though evil exists, I can choose to do what is right. When I do, you are pleased, good prevails, and Satan loses ground. I know that someday you will destroy the power of evil for all time. Until that day, may I fight evil by choosing to obey you and doing good.

Stay alert! Watch out for your great enemy, the devil. He prowls around like a roaring lion, looking for someone to devour. Stand firm against him, and be strong in your faith.
1 PETER 5:8-9

DAY 146 *Prayerful Moment*

✓ ### A prayer about APPRECIATION
When I need to express my appreciation to others

MERCIFUL GOD,
I can still remember some of the encouraging words others have said to me. Whether they came through a note from a friend, a kind word from a teacher, or a conversation with a mentor, those words showed that someone noticed me, appreciated me, and saw potential in me. Father, those around me need words of appreciation and encouragement too. Please open my eyes to opportunities to build others up. May my words bless others.

I have not stopped thanking God for you. I pray for you constantly. EPHESIANS 1:16

✓ ## DAY 147 *Prayerful Moment*

A prayer about CELEBRATION
When my heart is full of rejoicing

MOST GLORIOUS LORD,
We celebrate earthly milestones such as birthdays, marriages, and births. But you have given me the best reason of all to celebrate: you have rescued me from the consequences of sin and shown me the way to heaven! When I celebrate, I take my focus off my problems and put it on you and your blessings. I praise you because I have so much to celebrate!

Let us be glad and rejoice. . . . For the time has come for the wedding feast of the Lamb. REVELATION 19:7

DAY 148

A prayer about the POWER OF GOD

When I marvel at how God's power has worked in me

LORD JESUS,

You are the one who could instantly calm the storm on the Sea of Galilee—and you have the power to calm the storms in my heart. You can dry up a flood of fear, quench my thirst for sin, and control the whirlwind of my life. I have seen your miracles, Jesus, and I've experienced your work in my heart. My life is a living demonstration of your powerful work! May I never keep this story to myself, but may I take every opportunity to tell others what you have done in me. I praise you that I am not the woman I used to be. You did not leave me in my struggles, but you came alongside me with your miraculous power and began to transform my life. May you be glorified.

[Jesus said,] "You will receive power when the Holy Spirit comes upon you. And you will be my witnesses, telling people about me everywhere . . . to the ends of the earth."

ACTS 1:8

A prayer about ATTITUDE
When I want to have the attitude of Christ

FATHER GOD,

I know that my attitude plays a huge role in how I view life. My attitude affects my actions; what I think about something often determines whether I will do anything about it. But you're showing me that my actions, inversely, can affect my attitude. Choosing to act the right way will eventually help me to think the right way. My circumstances will sometimes be pleasant and sometimes be difficult, but teach me that the way I react to them is almost more important than the circumstances themselves. Renew my mind, Lord, and enable me to respond with joy and humility to whatever happens, as Jesus did.

You must have the same attitude that Christ Jesus had. Though he was God, he did not think of equality with God as something to cling to. Instead, he gave up his divine privileges; he took the humble position of a slave and was born as a human being. When he appeared in human form, he humbled himself in obedience to God and died a criminal's death on a cross. PHILIPPIANS 2:5-8

A prayer about CHARACTER
When I want to develop godly character

LOVING GOD,

I want to be a woman of godly character. As I observe other Christians, I see that there is nothing more beautiful than a woman who is at peace with you and confident in the abilities and tasks you have given her. She knows her value in your eyes and rests in your love. She meets the needs of those around her, and that is appealing. Lord, may I cultivate inward beauty. May I focus my attention on eternal matters and on what you say is most important. Then the beauty of my actions and attitude will encourage others.

Even if some refuse to obey the Good News, your godly lives will speak to them without any words. They will be won over by observing your pure and reverent lives. Don't be concerned about the outward beauty of fancy hairstyles, expensive jewelry, or beautiful clothes. You should clothe yourselves instead with the beauty that comes from within, the unfading beauty of a gentle and quiet spirit, which is so precious to God. 1 PETER 3:1-4

DAY 151

✓ A prayer about COMFORT
When I need to experience God's comfort

HEAVENLY FATHER,
I am so thankful that you welcome me when I call on you in distress. Your Word tells me that you always answer the cry of those who are lonely, afraid, or brokenhearted, and I'm crying out to you right now. You are my comfort, Lord, and I cling to the promises you have set forth in your Word. May they encourage me in my circumstances and give me the confident assurance that I will one day live forever in peace and security with you. I praise you that your Word is as close as my fingertips, and you are as close as my whispered prayer.

The LORD hears his people when they call to him for help. He rescues them from all their troubles. The LORD is close to the brokenhearted; he rescues those whose spirits are crushed. PSALM 34:17-18

A prayer about COMMITMENT
When I ponder what it means to belong to God

LORD GOD,

You are my heavenly Father, and I am your child. Yet there's another way you relate to me: you tell me that as a believer, I am part of your bride, the church. What an amazing promise! Your Word often uses marriage as an illustration for the holy relationship between you and your people. That's because both relationships—Father/child and marriage—are formed on the basis of a covenant, a holy promise, in which the parties will be faithful to each other exclusively. That image helps me to understand what it really means to be united with you. You are the one divine love of my life, and I have committed to loving, serving, and obeying you as long as I live and through eternity. I am filled with gratitude that you have called me to be part of the eternal relationship between Christ and his bride. As I think about this truth, I pray that the joy I find in my walk with you will grow and grow.

Praise the LORD! For the Lord our God, the Almighty, reigns. Let us be glad and rejoice, and let us give honor to him. For the time has come for the wedding feast of the Lamb, and his bride has prepared herself. REVELATION 19:6-7

DAY 153 *Prayerful Moment*

✓ A prayer about OBSTACLES

When I am facing overwhelming obstacles

LORD GOD,

My problems seem so big, but I cling to the promise that you, through the power of the Holy Spirit, have given me all I need to overcome whatever overwhelms me. You have already rescued me from sin's control and Satan's power! What could possibly be more difficult than that? When I remember that I am free from their rule, the problems of this world lose their grip on me.

[God the Father] has rescued us from the kingdom of darkness and transferred us into the Kingdom of his dear Son, who purchased our freedom and forgave our sins.

COLOSSIANS 1:13-14

DAY 154 *Prayerful Moment*

✓ A prayer about GOODNESS

When I desire to reflect God's goodness

LORD GOD,

You are good! Your goodness is displayed in your kindness, helpfulness, generosity, gentleness, mercy, and justice. Only you are truly good, but I want to reflect your nature, Lord. May those qualities be seen in me more and more as I allow you to take control of my heart.

The Kingdom of God is . . . a matter of . . . living a life of goodness and peace and joy in the Holy Spirit.

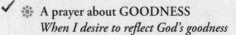

ROMANS 14:17

A prayer about GOD'S TIMING

When God seems slow to act

HEAVENLY FATHER,

Oh, how I hate to wait! When I get stuck at a red light or in a slow line at the grocery store, I often become impatient and edgy. And when you don't seem to be acting in my life, even when it's clear that the thing I've prayed for is right and good, I get frustrated. Lord, it's hard to accept that your timing is different from mine. It's even harder to accept that your timing is best for me because I can't see what's up ahead. I want what seems best for me now! But I do trust you, and I want to act in a way that reflects that trust. I know that when I wait on you, I'm showing confidence in the fulfillment of your promises for my life, now and in the future. Teach me to wait quietly for you to act, without becoming restless or agitated. Grant me patience to wait for your timing.

I am confident I will see the LORD's goodness while I am here in the land of the living. Wait patiently for the LORD. Be brave and courageous. Yes, wait patiently for the LORD.

PSALM 27:13-14

✓ ## A prayer about the PAST
When I'm haunted by my past

LORD GOD,
I know that the way I view my past will affect how I live now and in the future. Some aspects of my past are good. Thank you for the spiritual heritage I have received from family and mentors. May I use it to help others and never take it for granted. But some parts of my past are painful, Lord. Difficult things happened that wounded me. I'm also filled with regret for actions of my own that were wrong and hurtful. Thank you that no matter what I've done or what has been done to me, you are ready to heal me, cleanse me, and give me a fresh start. I humbly ask you to redeem my past and restore me. I believe you can remove my regret, guilt, and shame. Thank you, Lord! May I no longer be a slave to my past. Free me to live in peace with purpose and joy.

Fear not; you will no longer live in shame. Don't be afraid; there is no more disgrace for you. You will no longer remember the shame of your youth. ISAIAH 54:4

A prayer about SUFFERING
When someone I love is suffering

MERCIFUL GOD,
It's a sad reflection on our broken world that suffering is a universal experience. I know that some suffering, such as illness, comes simply as a result of living in a fallen world. Other suffering happens as a result of sin, if we stubbornly go against your commands and then suffer the consequences. Whatever the source, everyone on earth has felt the dark shadow of suffering. Someone I love is struggling now and wondering why, and I don't know what to say. Help me, Lord, to accept the fact that often I will not know why suffering has struck. Keep me from trying to explain it out of my ignorance. Instead, equip me to join in my loved one's suffering—to choose to be wounded with my friend and so to bring comfort. Give me the strength to walk alongside, to point the suffering one to you, and to bring comfort and hope.

All praise to God, the Father of our Lord Jesus Christ. God is our merciful Father and the source of all comfort. He comforts us in all our troubles so that we can comfort others. When they are troubled, we will be able to give them the same comfort God has given us. 2 CORINTHIANS 1:3-4

A prayer about DISTRACTIONS
When I'm facing a new distraction

FATHER GOD,

So often I see new things that come my way as distractions from serving you. But I'm reminded of Paul and Silas when they were thrown in jail in Philippi. They didn't chafe at the situation, frustrated because incarceration was keeping them from their missionary work. Instead, they saw this situation as a new way to serve you! They didn't push away their distraction but embraced it—and as a result they saw you work in a mighty way. Father, please give me wisdom to see what you would have me do with whatever new distraction appears in my life. Have you put it in my path to help me focus on who is right in front of me needing help? Or what you want me to do? May I follow your call to minister, whether you're asking me to keep on with what I've been doing or calling me to new people in a new place.

The jailer called for lights and ran to the dungeon and fell down trembling before Paul and Silas. Then he brought them out and asked, "Sirs, what must I do to be saved?" They replied, "Believe in the Lord Jesus and you will be saved. . . ." And they shared the word of the Lord with him and with all who lived in his household. ACTS 16:29-32

A prayer about FAITH

When I want to strengthen my faith

FATHER,

I know that I can't increase my faith merely by my own effort. Faith is divinely inspired by your Holy Spirit, who often works through your Word. My faith grows as I read the stories of your work through people across the centuries and realize you can do the same through me. I need to believe even when I cannot see; after all, the strongest faith is not one based on physical senses but on spiritual conviction. I ask you to sharpen my "spiritual vision" so I can see the results of your work in my life and in the lives of those around me. Teach me to be more aware of your active presence in the world so that my faith will grow. I know that without faith, it's impossible to please you.

[Jesus] said to Thomas, "Put your finger here, and look at my hands. Put your hand into the wound in my side. Don't be faithless any longer. Believe!" "My Lord and my God!" Thomas exclaimed. Then Jesus told him, "You believe because you have seen me. Blessed are those who believe without seeing me." JOHN 20:27-29

DAY 160 *Prayerful Moment*

✓ A prayer about ENTHUSIASM
When I want to work with energy

LORD JESUS,
When I do my work as if I were doing it for you, I can work with more enthusiasm because my tasks are infused with a sense of divine purpose. I want to please you with my work, not just get through the task. Help me to imitate your approach and attitude. May my efforts influence those around me for your glory.

Work with enthusiasm, as though you were working for the Lord rather than for people. EPHESIANS 6:7

DAY 161 *Prayerful Moment*

✓ A prayer about COMPLACENCY
When I've lost my passion for following God

O LORD,
I've lost my excitement for following you. I'm feeling apathetic toward the things of your Kingdom, and I think I know why. Sin has gotten a foothold in my life, and it's leading me away from you. I confess that sin, Lord. Please forgive me. I know that Satan will use all his power to keep me from being excited about following you, but you are stronger than Satan. Draw me back to you and reignite my passion.

We must listen very carefully to the truth we have heard, or we may drift away from it. HEBREWS 2:1

A prayer about SIGNIFICANCE
When I want my life to count

LORD GOD,

Deep within my heart is a yearning for my life to count, to make a difference, to be worth something. Sometimes I struggle with feeling insignificant—I'm not sure I'm doing anything truly important. I become paralyzed by what I cannot do rather than acting on what I can do. Everywhere I look I see others who are more successful, more beautiful, more gifted, more this, more that. But you have shown me through your Word that the heroes of the faith—people such as Moses, Rahab, Esther, and Peter—were ordinary people who learned that their significance came not from what *they* could accomplish with their abilities, but from what *you* could accomplish through their abilities. Imprint this truth on my heart, Lord. You have created me, and you have given me gifts and talents that you want me to use for your purpose. When I do that, no matter how I compare with anyone else, my life will become significant, both now and for eternity.

My life is worth nothing to me unless I use it for finishing the work assigned me by the Lord Jesus—the work of telling others the Good News about the wonderful grace of God.

ACTS 20:24

A prayer about CONFUSION
When I'm uncertain about the future

LORD GOD,

Sometimes I feel confused about which direction I should take. It's frustrating to waver, full of indecision. But I know that your Word gives me a sure compass and directs me the right way. I can begin to reduce the confusion in my life when I follow the Bible's guidelines about what roads *not* to take. When I'm doubting my path, help me to read your Word, focus my thoughts on you, and pray for your wisdom. Show me which paths are off-limits and which is the right one for me. You promise to direct me as I seek your will, and I cling to that promise. Clear up my confusion as you teach me to view the world from your perspective. May I never rely on myself but depend solely on your wisdom.

Trust in the LORD with all your heart; do not depend on your own understanding. Seek his will in all you do, and he will show you which path to take. PROVERBS 3:5-6

✓ A prayer about INVOLVEMENT
When I don't want to get involved with another's problems

HEAVENLY FATHER,

It's all too easy for me to see a problem and think, *I don't want to get involved.* Maybe the situation looks too messy or complicated, or I'm not sure my help would be appreciated. I'm sometimes tempted to pretend I don't notice the problem, hoping that someone else will take care of it. But you call me to be compassionate and active, ready and willing to go the extra mile. You command me to love my neighbor as I love myself—and that's a call to action. Please give me the courage to get involved. May I respond, not just when it's convenient, but whenever you provide an opportunity. Allow me the privilege of sharing your love with someone who needs help through a difficult situation.

If you see your neighbor's ox or sheep or goat wandering away, don't ignore your responsibility. Take it back to its owner. . . . Do the same if you find your neighbor's donkey, clothing, or anything else your neighbor loses. Don't ignore your responsibility. DEUTERONOMY 22:1, 3

A prayer about CHALLENGES
When I'm afraid to take risks

LORD GOD,

I'm facing new challenges, and meeting them will require me to take some risks. That's scary for me, but when I look at your Word, I see many examples of great risk takers who embraced the challenges of their lives. Abram left everyone and everything he knew when he responded to your call to move to a new place. Esther risked her life to go before the king and plead for the Jewish people. These were ordinary people, but you empowered them to respond to big challenges. Make me bold, Lord! As I take risks for you, may I have faith that you are by my side and will help me overcome whatever I am facing. Give me the courage to step out boldly in confidence. I know you will open the way for me.

In [the LORD's] strength I can crush an army; with my God I can scale any wall. . . . For who is God except the LORD? Who but our God is a solid rock? God is my strong fortress, and he makes my way perfect.

2 SAMUEL 22:30, 32-33

DAY 166

A prayer about EXCELLENCE

When I ponder why I need to give my best to God

HEAVENLY FATHER,

I know that what I value reflects the condition of my heart. When I give you my best, I show how much I value my relationship with you. But too often my actions show that I am not truly putting you first in my life. When I give you only what is left of my income, I'm showing that I value money more than you. When I spend time with you only when it's convenient, I'm communicating that I value other things more than time with you. Forgive me for trying to get away with less than my best. You have given only the best to me—salvation and eternal life through the death and resurrection of Christ! I pray for the commitment to put you first, to give you my best instead of my leftovers. May my choices reflect my love for you. I know you will bless me for it.

In all that he did in the service of the Temple of God and in his efforts to follow God's laws and commands, Hezekiah sought his God wholeheartedly. As a result, he was very successful. 2 CHRONICLES 31:21

DAY 167 *Prayerful Moment*

✓ A prayer about WORRY
When I'm overcome with worry

FATHER GOD,
My circumstances are overwhelming me, but by your strength I will refuse to worry. When bad situations come my way, I need your help to turn my fears into confident prayer. I bring my needs to you in thanksgiving for what you have already done, and I trust that you will bring fruit out of these difficult times.

Don't worry about anything; instead, pray about everything. Tell God what you need, and thank him for all he has done.
PHILIPPIANS 4:6

✓ DAY 168 *Prayerful Moment*

A prayer about CARING
When I desire to help others

LORD,
Your very nature is to care for others, and I am made in your image. Please move my heart with compassion for those around me who are in need. May I be willing to provide for others, share with them, comfort them, or just be present with them. I want to please you, Lord, and I want to reflect your nature in the way I exhibit compassion for others.

The King will say, "I tell you the truth, when you did it to one of the least of these my brothers and sisters, you were doing it to me!" MATTHEW 25:40

DAY 169

A prayer about HOLINESS
When I wonder how I can live a holy life

LORD GOD,

You alone are holy, yet you also call me to be holy. To be completely holy is to be sinless, pure, and perfect. I'll never attain that in this lifetime, but it's my ultimate goal and, by faith, my final state—one I'll reach when I stand before you in heaven. I know this is possible only because I've been made righteous by Christ, and my heart is full of gratitude for your gracious gift. You call me to be holy, but you provide everything I need to become holy one day! O Lord, I know that being holy also means that you call me to be set apart for a specific purpose. By your grace I am different from the rest of the world, chosen to follow you and do your will. May I be diligent in this calling, making progress each day as I seek to become the woman you have created me to be.

I am writing . . . to you who have been called by God to be his own holy people. He made you holy by means of Christ Jesus, just as he did for all people everywhere who call on the name of our Lord Jesus Christ. 1 CORINTHIANS 1:2

DAY 170

A prayer about GOD'S CALL

When I reflect on how God pursues a relationship with me

LOVING GOD,

It's hard for me to comprehend your unconditional love, which pursues me no matter what I've done. I see this clearly in your Word. Adam and Eve disobeyed you and rebelled against you, yet the first thing you did was work to restore their relationship with you! They had to experience the consequences of their actions, but you acted with great love and sacrifice to keep the relationship from being severed. I praise you for your love, which is so great I can't even comprehend it. You never give up on me when I do what is wrong or even when I reject you. Instead, you pursue me for the purpose of forgiving my sin and restoring me. Teach me always to be sensitive to your Holy Spirit, who convicts me when I have sinned and leads me back to you. May I also be diligent about reading your Word, which calls me to confession and repentance. Lord, your faithful pursuit is a beautiful call to friendship with me. I pray that I will always respond to it.

Long ago the LORD said to Israel: "I have loved you, my people, with an everlasting love. With unfailing love I have drawn you to myself." JEREMIAH 31:3

A prayer about LISTENING
When I want to become a good listener

HEAVENLY FATHER,

I want to be a better listener—both to you and to those around me. Too often I try to do things my own way. I don't take advantage of godly counsel or ask questions that would help me gain understanding, and then I miss out on the wisdom you have for me. Help me, Lord, to be open to advice and even godly correction when I make mistakes. When I am willing to hear and learn, I mature spiritually and gain the knowledge to make decisions that please you. I know that being a good listener also means talking less and choosing my words carefully when I do speak. I don't want to hurt others with my thoughtless words. Please work in my heart and help me to develop self-control. As I listen with greater care, may those around me be encouraged to share their thoughts with me. I pray for the humility and maturity to respond with love and wisdom.

If you reject discipline, you only harm yourself; but if you listen to correction, you grow in understanding.

PROVERBS 15:32

A prayer about GOD'S PROMISES
When I affirm my belief in God's promises

FAITHFUL LORD,
When other people promise me something, I consider whether they are truthful and dependable and whether they have the ability to carry out what they promised. I'm really assessing their character and power. But the truth is, only you possess both of these in perfect degree. You alone are completely trustworthy; I trust you absolutely. Lord, I believe that your promises will come true, even when my circumstances lead me to doubt. Your word is rock solid; your promises will never falter or waver. I have all the reassurance I need, and I give you my heart.

I bow before your holy Temple as I worship. I praise your name for your unfailing love and faithfulness; for your promises are backed by all the honor of your name.
PSALM 138:2

A prayer about ACCEPTANCE
When I ponder that God really accepts me

HEAVENLY FATHER,

Romans 3:23 makes it clear that every person on earth has sinned and fallen short of your standard. Nothing I could ever do would make me worthy of you. Yet the miracle is that you accept me as your child! Out of your great love, you gave your Son to die for me—before I was even born or had ever committed a sin. You have always been there, waiting for me to receive your forgiveness, and then you welcomed me into your presence! When I realize how fully you accept me, I am freed from the terrible burden of trying to earn your love. Thank you for this miraculous freedom. I am overwhelmed with praise and gratitude.

God showed how much he loved us by sending his one and only Son into the world so that we might have eternal life through him. This is real love—not that we loved God, but that he loved us and sent his Son as a sacrifice to take away our sins. 1 JOHN 4:9-10

DAY 174 *Prayerful Moment*

✓ A prayer about MEDITATION
When I want to improve my spiritual focus

LORD,
Teach me to set aside time to think about you, talk to you, and listen to you. Help me to remove myself from the noise of the world around me and move within range of your voice. I want to hear you, Lord. Prepare me to be teachable; may I allow you to mold my desires into what you desire. I know you can bring my thoughts and actions in line with your will as I focus on you.

Be still, and know that I am God! PSALM 46:10

DAY 175 *Prayerful Moment*

✓ A prayer about WORDS
When I consider how my words affect others

LOVING GOD,
Let me never get careless and speak as though my words are unimportant. I know that the things I say have enormous impact on those who hear. May what I say never be annoying, complaining, insulting, or demeaning. Instead, help me to choose my words carefully and make them count. Teach me to encourage, inspire, comfort, and challenge those around me. Guide and guard my lips.

Let everything you say be good and helpful, so that your words will be an encouragement to those who hear them.
EPHESIANS 4:29

A prayer about INTEGRITY
When I want to be a woman of integrity

HEAVENLY FATHER,

It has been said that integrity is essentially the unity between my character and yours. When my character mirrors yours, my heart, mind, and actions will be pure, reflecting your nature. I long to reach that point, but I often fall short. My character takes center stage and I act in ways that disappoint you. How can I develop more integrity? I want to achieve it instantly, but the truth is that it's a process. Just as fire is necessary for refining gold, you are refining me through the heat of pressure and troubles. Help me to look at every day as a refining process that tests how pure I am becoming. May I not complain about the trials that come but welcome them, knowing that they are forming my character. As I develop in integrity, may I thank you for giving me the power, privilege, and direction to live according to your ways.

[The Lord said,] "I will bring that group through the fire and make them pure. I will refine them like silver and purify them like gold. They will call on my name, and I will answer them. I will say, 'These are my people,' and they will say, 'The LORD is our God.'" ZECHARIAH 13:9

A prayer about SURPRISE
When I'm surprised by God

HOLY GOD,
You never change, yet when I read the Bible, I see that you often do the opposite of what I would expect. You chose the youngest son of Jesse, David, rather than the oldest to be king of Israel. You took Saul, the most vicious opponent of the early church, and transformed him into Paul, the most courageous missionary of all time. You cared for and respected women in a time when they had no rights. And you used crucifixion, the symbol of ultimate defeat, and made it the sign of victory over sin and death for all eternity. I praise you because your creativity and ingenuity know no boundaries. May I never limit you to the horizon of my own understanding and expectations. Teach me to perceive what you are doing all around me. When I'm surprised by the amazing ways you work, may I respond with awe, love, gratitude, and joy.

[Jesus] gave up his divine privileges; he took the humble position of a slave and was born as a human being. When he appeared in human form, he humbled himself in obedience to God and died a criminal's death on a cross. Therefore, God elevated him to the place of highest honor and gave him the name above all other names. PHILIPPIANS 2:7-9

A prayer about SATISFACTION
When I feel discontented with my life

LORD,

Sometimes I try to meet my deepest needs in ways that just don't satisfy. When I feel a hunger in my soul, too often I turn to fun, pleasure, or busyness to distract me. These things aren't necessarily bad, but they will never fill my cravings. Only you can satisfy. You created me to be in relationship with you, and when I don't make that relationship a priority, I will be dissatisfied. Teach me to recognize my soul cravings for what they are, and to respond to them by spending time with you and your Word. May your Holy Spirit fill me with what I need to make me a strong and mature believer. You are the Living Water, and those who drink from you will never thirst again. Fill me with yourself, Lord. Then I know that I will find the satisfaction that comes directly from you.

Jesus [said], "Anyone who drinks this water will soon become thirsty again. But those who drink the water I give will never be thirsty again. It becomes a fresh, bubbling spring within them, giving them eternal life." JOHN 4:13-14

✓ A prayer about CIRCUMSTANCES
When I'm in difficult situations and need to experience God

LORD,
The more I wallow in the difficulty of unpleasant circumstances, the more I feel dragged under. I need you to rescue me! I reach out to you, knowing that when I do, you lift me up. You are with me always, and you have given me the eternal gift of salvation. How can I not respond to you with joy, even in my difficulties? Help me to focus less on my troubles and more on the joy, peace, and future that come from a relationship with you. Teach me to praise you in the midst of trials, and open my eyes to see your blessings.

Though the fig trees have no blossoms, and there are no grapes on the vines; even though the olive crop fails, and the fields lie empty and barren; even though the flocks die in the fields, and the cattle barns are empty, yet I will rejoice in the LORD*! I will be joyful in the God of my salvation! The Sovereign* LORD *is my strength! He makes me as surefooted as a deer, able to tread upon the heights.*
HABAKKUK 3:17-19

A prayer about TENDERNESS

When I want to feel more tenderness toward others

O GOD,

You care for me with tenderness and compassion. Your Word—in Isaiah 49:14-15—compares your love for your people to that of a nursing mother tending to her baby and—in Matthew 23:37—that of a mother hen protecting her chicks. You are the God of the universe, the King over all creation, yet your heart is filled with mercy for me! May I reflect your heart in the way I treat other people. My heart has been hardened and dulled by years of sin. Please replace it with a soft and tender heart—plant a compassionate spirit within me. As I care for others, grant me moments when I realize the depth of your care for me. May my newly tender heart become ever more grateful for the many ways in which you have showered your love on me.

I will give you a new heart, and I will put a new spirit in you. I will take out your stony, stubborn heart and give you a tender, responsive heart. And I will put my Spirit in you so that you will follow my decrees and be careful to obey my regulations. EZEKIEL 36:26-27

DAY 181 *Prayerful Moment*

A prayer about ROLE MODELS
When I am inspired by another believer

LORD GOD,

Thank you for the role models in my life, especially those women who have inspired passion for you. I'm grateful for godly mentors, teachers, and friends who have opened my eyes to the wonderful blessings of serving you and walking in your ways. Thank you for putting these people in my path. I pray that someday my faith might inspire others to find their joy in you, as well.

Every time I think of you, I give thanks to my God.
PHILIPPIANS 1:3

DAY 182 *Prayerful Moment*

A prayer about QUIETNESS
When I wonder how times of quiet can help me

FATHER GOD,

You have blessed me with times that are free from pressures and temptations. Thank you for these quiet moments. I don't want to waste them—use them to strengthen me for the trials ahead. Increase my self-discipline, endurance, and faith, that I may have the spiritual wisdom and commitment to honor you in the face of intense struggles.

This is what the Sovereign LORD, *the Holy One of Israel, says: "Only in returning to me and resting in me will you be saved. In quietness and confidence is your strength."*
ISAIAH 30:15

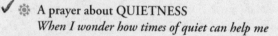

DAY 183

A prayer about HEAVEN
When I look forward to eternal life

ETERNAL GOD,

I often wonder what eternity with you will be like. In your Word, you have revealed just enough about heaven to give me something to anticipate with joy. I know I still have struggles to go through before I get there at the end of this life, but I am eager to see what you have planned. You have promised moments of joy; times of rest; the end of suffering; and, best of all, your presence. Thank you that because I have accepted Jesus' sacrifice on my behalf, you have redeemed me and I can anticipate this glorious promise!

With eager hope, the creation looks forward to the day when it will join God's children in glorious freedom from death and decay. For we know that all creation has been groaning as in the pains of childbirth right up to the present time. And we believers also groan, even though we have the Holy Spirit within us as a foretaste of future glory, for we long for our bodies to be released from sin and suffering. We, too, wait with eager hope for the day when God will give us our full rights as his adopted children, including the new bodies he has promised us. ROMANS 8:20-23

DAY 184

A prayer about CRITICISM
When I disapprove of others' choices

JESUS,
Sometimes the people around me make choices that blatantly go against your laws. I can't help disapproving, but I don't always know how to respond. It's tempting to lecture or to withdraw, but I don't think either choice is what you would have me do. After all, you focused on finding those who were furthest from you and ministering to their needs. I want to follow your example, and that means looking past people's behavior to their soul. I need your help for this, Lord Jesus. Open my eyes to see that these are the people who most need a godly friend. May I not turn away in judgment; rather, may I reach out and serve them in love.

When Jesus came by, he looked up at Zacchaeus and called him by name. "Zacchaeus!" he said. "Quick, come down! I must be a guest in your home today." Zacchaeus quickly climbed down and took Jesus to his house in great excitement and joy. But the people were displeased. "He has gone to be the guest of a notorious sinner," they grumbled. . . . Jesus responded, "Salvation has come to this home today. . . . For the Son of Man came to seek and save those who are lost."
LUKE 19:5-7, 9-10

A prayer about AMAZEMENT

When I want to recapture my sense of awe at what God has done

LORD GOD,

I have heard the Bible stories so many times that I have lost some of my initial sense of amazement. I'm ashamed to say it, but the miraculous things you have done in history sometimes seem almost routine. I need to regain my perspective so I can remember again how wonderful you are. Help me to pay attention to the world around me and see how you are working—in big ways and small. Give me ears to hear stories of how you have amazed others and entered into their lives in tangible ways. Show me the beauties of creation around me, the blessing of close friendships, the miracle of people sharing your love. Feeling awe over these everyday miracles will prepare my heart to experience even more astounding things. As I look around me and read your Word, may I always look for evidence of your work. I know I will find it and be amazed.

O God, your ways are holy. Is there any god as mighty as you? You are the God of great wonders! You demonstrate your awesome power among the nations. PSALM 77:13-14

A prayer about DISCIPLINE
When I need to learn better self-control

LORD,

You ask me to exercise self-control over what I think, what I say, and what I do. But often this seems impossible! I'm undisciplined and I constantly slip. I need your transforming help. May I learn your guidelines for right living, which you communicate through your Word. Teach me also to be aware of my weaknesses and alert to times when I am likely to be tempted. Thank you for the Holy Spirit, who lives in me and will help me stand strong against temptation when I ask. The Bible tells me that you always provide a way out when I face temptation; please give me the strength to choose it. When I slip up, may I not run from you but toward you, confessing my sin and asking for your forgiveness and continued help. And in those wonderful times when I am victorious, may I always give you the glory!

The temptations in your life are no different from what others experience. And God is faithful. He will not allow the temptation to be more than you can stand. When you are tempted, he will show you a way out so that you can endure. 1 CORINTHIANS 10:13

DAY 187

A prayer about VULNERABILITY

When I wonder if I can trust God with my deepest secrets

LORD GOD,

What if others knew who I really am? That thought frightens me. I'm not sure there's anyone to whom I can reveal my true self: my deepest fears, hurts, sins, or doubts. I need that kind of intimacy, but I resist it because it requires vulnerability—and that means revealing the dark things I hoped would never come out into the open. O God, I even resist being vulnerable with you about my sins, especially the ones I don't want to give up. But you require full disclosure, and I know it's for my own good. Only through being vulnerable will I find true healing, restoration, renewal, and forgiveness. I desire that with all my heart. As I admit my sin and seek forgiveness, may my relationship with you be restored, and may I find a great weight lifted. I trust in your love for me, so I have nothing to fear and nothing to hide. You see my sin, you forgive me, and you are changing me.

Search me, O God, and know my heart; test me and know my anxious thoughts. Point out anything in me that offends you, and lead me along the path of everlasting life.
PSALM 139:23-24

DAY 188 *Prayerful Moment*

A prayer about ASSURANCE
When I think about heaven

FATHER,
I've entrusted my life to you, and I know you will guard my eternal future. Because I have that security, I can be strong and courageous as I seek to follow where you lead. I am confident in your promise of eternal life and a future beyond anything I can imagine. Help me to live today with that promise at the forefront of my mind. May it transform my perspective.

When the Great Shepherd appears, you will receive a crown of never-ending glory and honor. 1 PETER 5:4

DAY 189 *Prayerful Moment*

A prayer about GENTLENESS
When I want to learn to be gentle

HEAVENLY FATHER,
You are the perfect example of gentleness. Your Word tells me that you are as tender to your people as a mother to her infant, yet you are also a mighty warrior, able to defeat the powers of hell. As I encounter difficult situations with my family or coworkers, please help me to keep your example before me and remember that I can accomplish more with gentleness than with coercion.

Pursue righteousness and a godly life, along with faith, love, perseverance, and gentleness. 1 TIMOTHY 6:11

A prayer about APPROVAL

When I ponder how I have God's approval

LORD GOD,

I confess that whether I approve of others often comes down to their appearance or performance, even though I know it's shallow to look only at the outside. I'm blessed when I remember that your approval of me is based on your grace and unconditional love. Because I am your child, redeemed by Christ, you love me no matter what I do or how well I measure up. This doesn't mean you approve of my sinful behavior—that may have consequences. But you love me for who I am rather than for what I do. You created me in your image, and I am yours. I praise you for the amazing knowledge that nothing I do will cause you to love me any less. There's no way I can earn your approval, but through Christ I have your approval. May that motivate me to do all I can to please you.

I am convinced that nothing can ever separate us from God's love. Neither death nor life, neither angels nor demons, neither our fears for today nor our worries about tomorrow—not even the powers of hell can separate us from God's love. No power in the sky above or in the earth below—indeed, nothing in all creation will ever be able to separate us from the love of God that is revealed in Christ Jesus our Lord.

ROMANS 8:38-39

✓ A prayer about BELONGING

When I consider what it means to belong to God

LORD,

Because I belong to you, I know that sin no longer controls me. I still sin, of course, but I'm no longer enslaved to it—with your help I can overcome it because you have set me free from it! Because I belong to you, I can be certain that death is not the end. My heart overflows when I realize that I will live eternally with you and receive all that you have promised in the Bible. And because I belong to you, you bless me today with spiritual blessings, peace of heart, comfort, close friendships, and the satisfaction of knowing that I'm doing what you created me to do. Thank you, Lord, for these countless privileges that come from belonging to you and being part of your family!

All praise to God, the Father of our Lord Jesus Christ, who has blessed us with every spiritual blessing in the heavenly realms because we are united with Christ.

EPHESIANS 1:3

A prayer about DESIRES

When I need to evaluate my desires

LORD,

There are many things that I want, and those desires can be so strong! Sometimes, such as when I covet something that belongs to someone else, it's easy to see that my desires are wrong. At other times, such as when I want to know you more, it's easy to see that they are right. But for those times in the middle, when I'm not sure whether a desire is right or wrong, help me to consider the long-term consequences. Is what I want good, consistent with your Word, and helpful or at least harmless to others? If so, you give me the freedom to pursue it, with discernment. Above all, Lord, I long for the things you desire for me. Mold me and give me a hunger for good and honorable things. Teach me to fix my mind on what pleases you, knowing that my desires will follow.

Fix your thoughts on what is true, and honorable, and right, and pure, and lovely, and admirable. Think about things that are excellent and worthy of praise.

PHILIPPIANS 4:8

A prayer about SELF-ESTEEM
When I want to become a confident, secure woman

LORD,
Sometimes I feel trapped by my insecurities. I know that thinking more highly of myself than I should is pride, and I want to avoid that. But thinking less of myself than I should is false humility, and that's not ideal either. In between is self-esteem—an honest appraisal of my own worth based on who I am in you. Your Word makes clear that you value me highly because you love me deeply. Thank you that you are sufficient for me. I have worth because you place value on me and you have created me for a purpose. That makes me a woman of great value. May I believe this in my heart, and may it affect the way I live, freeing me from crippling insecurities and giving me the confidence to do what you have called me to do.

Not a single sparrow can fall to the ground without your Father knowing it. And the very hairs on your head are all numbered. So don't be afraid; you are more valuable to God than a whole flock of sparrows. MATTHEW 10:29-31

A prayer about PAIN

When I need to find hope during painful circumstances

HEAVENLY FATHER,

Pain is an almost constant part of life, whether it's physical—from a broken bone or failing health—or emotional—from betrayal, abandonment, or a broken relationship. I know that my greatest hope in times of pain is to turn to you for healing. Your Word assures me that you never take the day off; you never forget about me. When I feel as though you have abandoned me, it's often because I have become so focused on easing the hurt from my problems that I've forgotten you. You have not promised to remove my pain in this life, but you have promised to help me. Thank you, Lord, that you are always with me in my suffering. You give me hope and purpose in the midst of my aching body and soul.

We believers . . . groan, even though we have the Holy Spirit within us as a foretaste of future glory, for we long for our bodies to be released from sin and suffering. We . . . wait with eager hope for the day when God will give us our full rights as his adopted children, including the new bodies he has promised us. We were given this hope when we were saved. ROMANS 8:23-24

DAY 195 *Prayerful Moment*

A prayer about COMPASSION
When I want to reflect Christ's compassion

LORD JESUS,
When I see the incredible needs and pain around me, my heart aches. That gives me just an idea of how the needs of all humanity moved you to compassion and to action—dying on the cross for us. May my compassion go beyond emotion. May it motivate me to put my love into action to meet the needs of those around me.

Jesus saw the huge crowd as he stepped from the boat, and he had compassion on them because they were like sheep without a shepherd. MARK 6:34

DAY 196 *Prayerful Moment*

A prayer about ABILITIES
When I want to make the most of my abilities

FATHER,
I rejoice in the abilities you have given me! When I use them, I have a sense of satisfaction. I feel fulfilled. I know that my abilities give me the *potential* for doing good, but you give me the *power* to do good. Without you, my abilities are worthless. So may I pour out my rejoicing as an offering of thanks to you, the God who gave my abilities to me.

In his grace, God has given us different gifts for doing certain things well. ROMANS 12:6

A prayer about GUILT

When feelings of guilt keep me from believing that I am forgiven

FATHER,

Sometimes when I confess my sin to you, all seems well. But other times, even though I'm repentant and have laid my wrongs before you, I still feel guilty. Your Word, in 1 John 1:9, tells me that you are faithful to forgive my sins when I confess them, so I know that the problem is not with you but with me. I know that it's not your will for me to try to atone for my sin by feeling guilty and miserable. You have already cleansed me through Jesus' sacrifice! Please help me to trust that you forgive me. Like the immoral woman who washed your feet, may I accept your forgiveness by faith and respond with a life changed by gratitude. Thank you for freeing me to worship you gratefully, serve you humbly, and express my faith in you boldly.

When a certain immoral woman from that city heard [Jesus] was eating there, she brought a beautiful alabaster jar filled with expensive perfume. Then she knelt behind him at his feet, weeping. Her tears fell on his feet, and she wiped them off with her hair. Then she kept kissing his feet and putting perfume on them. . . . [Jesus said,] "I tell you, her sins—and they are many—have been forgiven, so she has shown me much love." LUKE 7:37-38, 47

A prayer about CRISIS
When I'm struggling with crisis

FATHER,
I love you, and I'm trying to serve you with my whole heart—yet I'm facing a time of crisis, and it's shaking me to the core. Sometimes I feel that doing your will should exempt me from this world's trials. After all, even Jesus' disciples seemed surprised when a dangerous storm threatened their lives while they were involved in your work. But even in their shock, they still knew where to turn for help: to Jesus, who was right there with them. You are with me, too! Just as Jesus awoke immediately when he heard the disciples' cries for help, so you hear me through all the noise and distractions of the world. I call out to you, asking for your care and protection. Please break through my fears and calm my heart. Help me to rest in your presence, even in this crisis and even though the storms of life continue to rage around me.

Call on me when you are in trouble, and I will rescue you, and you will give me glory. PSALM 50:15

DAY 199

A prayer about GOD'S PRESENCE
When I want to be more aware of God's presence

LORD,
Your Word tells me that you are with me always, but I'm embarrassed to say I sometimes forget that you are present. You are there, gently speaking to me, but so often I'm just not paying attention. Please forgive me, Lord. I want to live with a constant sense of your presence and in moment-by-moment conversation with you. Help me to be sensitive to reminders of your presence throughout the day. When those reminders come, I need to stop what I'm doing, remember that you have been with me in the previous hours, and ask you to help me in the hours ahead. I need to listen to you, not just talk. I'm so blessed to have you with me, and I want to be aware of this precious gift every moment.

I can never escape from your Spirit! I can never get away from your presence! If I go up to heaven, you are there; if I go down to the grave, you are there. If I ride the wings of the morning, if I dwell by the farthest oceans, even there your hand will guide me, and your strength will support me.
PSALM 139:7-10

✓ A prayer about SENSITIVITY

When I realize I've become dulled to the Holy Spirit's leading

FATHER GOD,

I'm beginning to realize that my spiritual sensitivity has been dulled. I used to be so aware of your leading and your voice, but when I look back at the past days I see that I've lost my keen awareness of your presence. What has changed? I know that many things can affect me this way: Sometimes this dullness happens when I've given up on fighting evil and instead have given in to sinful desires or compromised my convictions. Sometimes it occurs when I've spent too much time away from your truth, or have even actively ignored you. When I lack a fresh awareness of your holiness, I'm not sensitive to the sin in my life. O Lord, I know that if I want spiritual sensitivity, I must have eyes that are open to your Word and ears that are willing to hear it. Please renew my heart today. Forgive my slide into sin and teach me anew to listen carefully to your voice. May I always be sensitive to the leading of your Holy Spirit, and give me the courage to put that leading into action.

Open my eyes to see the wonderful truths in your instructions.
PSALM 119:18

A prayer about PERSEVERANCE
When I feel stretched to the breaking point

LORD GOD,
I don't know how much more I can bear, yet my situation has no quick fix. I need perseverance to get me through it. I know that you can deliver me from painful circumstances, but I also know that you often call your followers to a courageous and enduring faithfulness in the middle of trials. Strengthen me, Lord, so that I will not give up. May I not only endure this situation but overcome it with obedience, hope, and joy. If I can keep going and maintain my trust in you, I will be stronger in faith when I come out on the other side of this struggle. Give me a better understanding of the benefits of obeying you. Then I will develop greater confidence that when problems strike again, I can get through them—with your help.

Dear brothers and sisters, when troubles come your way, consider it an opportunity for great joy. For you know that when your faith is tested, your endurance has a chance to grow. So let it grow, for when your endurance is fully developed, you will be perfect and complete, needing nothing.
JAMES 1:2-4

DAY 202 *Prayerful Moment*

✓ A prayer about TESTING

When I need God to test my heart

ALL-KNOWING GOD,

You know me inside and out—my thoughts, my words, my actions, my motives. Examine my heart to discover what I value most. O Lord, forgive me for often making you an afterthought, giving you a minimum of my time or energy. Purify my heart so that the way I spend my time will reflect how much I value you.

Put me on trial, LORD, and cross-examine me. Test my motives and my heart. PSALM 26:2

✓ DAY 203 *Prayerful Moment*

A prayer about CREATIVITY

When I see God's creativity

CREATOR GOD,

All nature displays beauty that surpasses the finest music, poetry, and creative genius of all human artists put together. I praise you for being a God of design, color, plan, organization, beauty, magnificence, and order. All the great art of our world only copies your creation! Any creativity I have is the overflow of a heart and mind filled with your creative wonders.

The heavens proclaim the glory of God. The skies display his craftsmanship. Day after day they continue to speak; night after night they make him known. PSALM 19:1-2

A prayer about CRITICISM
When I'm facing criticism

MIGHTY GOD,
My pride is wounded right now because I've received criticism. I don't like to hear negative feedback from others, and I confess that my initial reaction is to ignore it. But I know your Word says that rejecting correction is foolish. If I want to be wise, I need to have a teachable heart. Help me, God, to view this criticism as a gift from you that might keep me from pursuing the wrong path. It can be painful to hear the truth, but it would be worse if I continued in harmful behavior. I want to get on the right track; I want to grow in my faith. I know you sometimes use the gentle rebuke of a trusted friend to get my attention and guide me. May I listen closely to you, Lord, so that you can help me discern wise correction. I always want to have a heart that is receptive to your leading.

Timely advice is lovely, like golden apples in a silver basket. To one who listens, valid criticism is like a gold earring or other gold jewelry. PROVERBS 25:11-12

✓ A prayer about ACCOMPLISHMENTS
When I wonder about my accomplishments

LORD,

Sometimes I assume that accomplishing great things is the way to become spiritually great. I feel as though I need to earn respect from others, impress others, and gain their approval. But that carries over to my relationship with you, and then I feel that I have to earn *your* love and forgiveness too. Impress on my heart, Lord, that I am accepted because of your grace, not because of what I accomplish. Romans 8:29-30 tells me that you accepted me even before I accomplished anything! What a reassuring truth. May I always understand that the good things I do are a result of your grace in me, not my own efforts. Release me from the bondage of needing to be accepted because of my performance, and free me to let you carry out your plans through me.

This Good News tells us how God makes us right in his sight. This is accomplished from start to finish by faith. As the Scriptures say, "It is through faith that a righteous person has life." ROMANS 1:17

DAY 206

A prayer about MISTAKES

When I'm weighed down by my mistakes

HEAVENLY FATHER,

I make so many mistakes, and sometimes I feel like giving up. How can you use me when I stumble so often? But in my discouragement, I remember the apostle Peter. Luke 22:31-34 explains that Jesus knew Peter would deny him, so Jesus prayed, asking first that Peter's mistakes would not cause him to lose his faith, and second, that Peter would eventually use the lessons he learned from his sins to strengthen others spiritually. You answered that prayer, Lord. I'm amazed when I read the book of Acts and see how you transformed Peter into the leader of your church in Jerusalem and an encourager of those suffering for their faith. I know that you can transform me, too. I may still face the heartache and consequences of my sin, yet in your wonderful grace you can use even my worst failures to strengthen my faith and enable me to better comfort and help others. May my mistakes never be wasted, Lord! Use them in my life so that I may bring glory to you.

The LORD directs the steps of the godly. He delights in every detail of their lives. Though they stumble, they will never fall, for the LORD holds them by the hand.

PSALM 37:23-24

✓ A prayer about NEIGHBORS
When I need to learn how to love my neighbor

LORD JESUS,

I think of my neighbors as the people who live next door or across the street, but you taught in the parable of the Good Samaritan that my neighbor is anyone around me who needs my love and care. That means that the person next to me on the plane, my coworkers, the other moms in the PTA, and the homeless people in my town are also my neighbors—as is anyone around the world who needs your love. How can I love all these people as I love myself? I need your help. Soften my heart and open my eyes. As I meet people around me, may I see these encounters as divinely appointed moments that allow me to share your grace. Help me to remember that it's not about *me* trying to do the right thing; instead, it's about pointing others to you, the source of all love.

Jesus [said], "The most important commandment is this: 'Listen, O Israel! The LORD our God is the one and only LORD. And you must love the LORD your God with all your heart, all your soul, all your mind, and all your strength.' The second is equally important: 'Love your neighbor as yourself.' No other commandment is greater than these."
MARK 12:29-31

A prayer about SIMPLICITY
When I want to simplify my life

FATHER,
How I desire a simpler life! Material things so quickly ensnare me, and I feel trapped. I need to pursue simplicity not just as a lifestyle but as a tangible expression of my heart. Help me, Lord, to develop the right attitudes. May I develop thankfulness, viewing every possession and good occurrence as a gift from you. Then I will expect nothing and find delight in everything. May I trust that my life and everything about it is ultimately under your care, not my own. Then I will be freed from anxiety and worry. And may I increase my generosity, being willing to share what I have with others. Teach me to hold things loosely, sharing my time and possessions as an expression of your generosity toward me. When I do this, I know you can free me from the slavery of materialism to live a life of simplicity, focused on you.

Jesus said, "That is why I tell you not to worry about everyday life—whether you have enough food to eat or enough clothes to wear. For life is more than food, and your body more than clothing." LUKE 12:22-23

DAY 209 *Prayerful Moment*

✓ A prayer about CIRCUMSTANCES
When I want to learn from the events of my life

FATHER,
My circumstances change all the time. But whether my life is filled with sunshine or with rain, you never change, and neither does your love for me. May I accept my circumstances with thanksgiving, and may I always trust you for your constant presence and comfort.

Devote yourselves to prayer with an alert mind and a thankful heart. COLOSSIANS 4:2

✓ DAY 210 *Prayerful Moment*

A prayer about CONVICTIONS
When I want my beliefs to affect my life

HOLY GOD,
I'm committed to the belief that Jesus is my Savior. Teach me always to live in such a way that convictions like this one are evident in what I think, say, and do. If I believe that you love me and created me, then out of this conviction should come the commitment to live by your Word, to serve others, and to fulfill your purpose for my life. May my convictions prepare me to live an effective life of faith, for your glory.

You must continue to believe this truth and stand firmly in it. Don't drift away from the assurance you received when you heard the Good News. COLOSSIANS 1:23

A prayer about SORROW
When I'm burdened with grief

MERCIFUL GOD,
I'm mourning a loss, and my grief is heavy upon me. I have moments when I'm overwhelmed with sadness and I can't think of anything else. Yet sometimes it seems that others feel I should be over my loss by now. I'm comforted by the example of Jeremiah, who in the book of Lamentations declared his grief in almost the same breath that he proclaimed his hope in your faithfulness. That shows me that the grief process is not intended to be swift, and it's not a steady progression. I'm reassured to know that tears and joy may be intermingled for a while. The best comfort is that you are with me, Lord, and that you care about my pain. Thank you for your promise that those who mourn will be comforted.

I will never forget this awful time, as I grieve over my loss. Yet I still dare to hope when I remember this: The faithful love of the LORD never ends! His mercies never cease. Great is his faithfulness; his mercies begin afresh each morning.
LAMENTATIONS 3:20-23

DAY 212

✓ A prayer about WITNESSING

When I consider how I can share God's love with others

ALMIGHTY GOD,

You call me, along with all other believers, to share the privilege and responsibility of being a witness to your love. This scares me sometimes, but the truth is that to witness simply means to tell about something I have experienced. And what I have experienced—the transforming power of your love for me—is so wonderful that I want to invite others to experience it too. Teach me always to be ready to tell about how I met you and grew to love you. May I be bold and faithful in my witness, never ashamed or afraid to tell others about you. Guide me to the people who need to hear my story. Perhaps someday I will have the privilege of knowing that your work in my life caused someone else to turn to you. May it be so!

God has not given us a spirit of fear and timidity, but of power, love, and self-discipline. So never be ashamed to tell others about our Lord. 2 TIMOTHY 1:7-8

✓ A prayer about my MOTIVES

When I want to have pure motives as I pursue God

HEAVENLY FATHER,

I know that my motives are of primary importance to you. The condition of my heart has a huge impact on the condition of my relationship with you. May I never come to you out of obligation or because I'm trying to get something I want. Instead, teach me always to come to you out of a humble desire to know you. I want to be driven by the desire to love you and please you, not by any selfish ambition. Help me to recognize that when my motives are wrong, my actions will be futile. When my motives are right, my actions will be meaningful and worthwhile. O Lord, when I pursue you with self-serving motives, I rob myself of the joy you intend me to have. Purify my heart so that I may seek you wholly and rightly.

I, the LORD, search all hearts and examine secret motives. I give all people their due rewards, according to what their actions deserve. JEREMIAH 17:10

DAY 214

A prayer about BROKENNESS
When I am grieving over my sin

HEAVENLY FATHER,
My circumstances are overwhelming. Sin has brought me low, and I realize that the only way out of my mess is through your help. I have hit bottom, and I understand as never before that I am utterly dependent on you. I am unrighteous; you are holy. I fail; you are perfect and all-sufficient. I have been trying to control my own life, but only you are really in control. Lord, please cast out my pride and make this mess be a turning point in my life. I release my life into your hands. Please forgive me and help me to repent fully. I ask you to draw close to me, heal my wounds, and restore me to you.

Have mercy on me, O God, because of your unfailing love. Because of your great compassion, blot out the stain of my sins. Wash me clean from my guilt. Purify me from my sin. For I recognize my rebellion; it haunts me day and night. Against you, and you alone, have I sinned; I have done what is evil in your sight. You will be proved right in what you say, and your judgment against me is just. PSALM 51:1-4

A prayer about DOUBT

When I ponder how God responds to my doubts

LORD JESUS,

I confess I am sometimes filled with doubt. In anxious moments, I doubt that you will really provide. When tragedy strikes, I doubt that you really care. In times of despair, I doubt that you are there at all. But you have promised in your Word that if I seek you, I will find you, and I cling to your promise. Thank you for the example of John the Baptist, who struggled with doubts about whether you were really the Messiah. You were gracious to reassure him, and I sense that compassion extended to me as well. Bring me through my times of doubting with a deeper faith, a better understanding of you, and a greater trust in your goodness. In my doubting, may I not sin against you—I never want my doubts to lead me into cynicism or hard-heartedness. Rather, may they always lead me to trust you more fully.

John the Baptist, who was in prison, heard about all the things the Messiah was doing. So he sent his disciples to ask Jesus, "Are you the Messiah we've been expecting, or should we keep looking for someone else?" Jesus told them, "Go back to John and tell him what you have heard and seen—the blind see, the lame walk, the lepers are cured, the deaf hear, the dead are raised to life, and the Good News is being preached to the poor." MATTHEW 11:2-5

DAY 216 *Prayerful Moment*

✓ A prayer about APPROVAL

When God's approval gives me new energy

LORD,

I am rejuvenated today because I know I am following your way, and I know you are pleased with my actions! I rejoice in your approval. May it stimulate me to even greater obedience. I am grateful for the opportunity to play a part in your Kingdom work.

Work hard so you can present yourself to God and receive his approval. Be a good worker, one who does not need to be ashamed and who correctly explains the word of truth. 2 TIMOTHY 2:15

✓

DAY 217 *Prayerful Moment*

A prayer about DISCERNMENT

When I want to grow in wisdom

LORD GOD,

My life can be confusing. I need your wisdom to help me through the maze of options I face. Please give me your discernment so that I may have the ability to differentiate between right and wrong, true and false, important and trivial, godly and ungodly. Just as the sun burns away the fog, cut through the confusion, I pray, and bring me clarity.

Let those who are wise understand these things. Let those with discernment listen carefully. The paths of the LORD *are true and right, and righteous people live by walking in them.*

HOSEA 14:9

DAY 218

✓ A prayer about BLESSINGS
When I want to experience God's blessings

LORD GOD,
When I read your Word, I see a recurring principle: obedience to you brings blessing, and disobedience brings misfortune. Sometimes I think about blessings only in terms of material things, but I know that the greatest things you give are far more valuable than money or possessions. You bless me by giving me joy, peace of heart, spiritual gifts, family, friendships, and the confidence of eternal life. Oh, Lord, you have given me far more than I often realize. I can't earn your gifts and I don't deserve them, but you give them freely because you love me. Thank you! My heart overflows with gratitude, and that calls me to ever greater obedience. Guard me from straying away from what is right; keep me always close to you, in the center of your blessing.

The LORD God is our sun and our shield. He gives us grace and glory. The LORD will withhold no good thing from those who do what is right. O LORD of Heaven's Armies, what joy for those who trust in you. PSALM 84:11-12

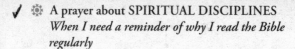

A prayer about SPIRITUAL DISCIPLINES
When I need a reminder of why I read the Bible regularly

FATHER,

I sometimes get tired of praying and reading the Bible. I'm ashamed to say that, Lord, especially because I know that doing those things regularly will bring extraordinary results. When I practice spiritual disciplines, I'm learning to avoid sin. But even more, I'm training myself to live with virtue and discipline. The more I practice these things, the more they will become second nature. When I pray and read your Word, I'm acknowledging that you are the source of all wisdom. I'm submitting myself to you because I know that your way is best. Please give me the self-discipline to keep on with daily Bible study, prayer, memorizing Scripture, and service. The more I do, with your help, the more I will resemble Jesus and live with integrity and purity. I want to strive for excellence in my walk with you. May I bring you glory.

How can a young person stay pure? By obeying your word. I have tried hard to find you—don't let me wander from your commands. I have hidden your word in my heart, that I might not sin against you. PSALM 119:9-11

✓ A prayer about SALVATION
When I want salvation to make a difference in my daily life

LORD GOD,

I'm amazed by the wonderful things you have promised me. When I received salvation by accepting Christ as Lord, you guaranteed that I would inherit eternal life in heaven. Everything I could want or need will be provided for me; I will lack for nothing and be forever in your presence. How wonderful! May this knowledge change the way I live now. Show me that when I possess eternal security, I can worry less. I can be confident that nothing can harm my soul or my future. I can take risks by stepping out in faith when I think you are asking me to do something for you. I can give generously and have peace of mind. O Lord, may I live as though my future holds everything I could ever want—because you have promised that it truly does.

We know that our old sinful selves were crucified with Christ so that sin might lose its power in our lives. We are no longer slaves to sin. For when we died with Christ we were set free from the power of sin. And since we died with Christ, we know we will also live with him. ROMANS 6:6-8

DAY 221

✓ A prayer about DECISIONS

When I wonder how my decisions make a difference in my walk with God

HEAVENLY FATHER,

Sometimes the little decisions in my life don't seem too important. But I know that each right decision puts me a little further down the path you want me to travel—the path of knowing you and being conformed to your likeness. I don't want to go astray. May I be faithful in the little things, because that will keep me in the center of your will. When I'm obeying you, serving others, reading your Word, and doing what is right, I will make good decisions. And doing all those things will draw me closer to you and cause me to be more sensitive to your leading in my life. In the little decisions and the big ones, may I press on to know you and to be faithful to you.

Oh, that we might know the LORD! Let us press on to know him. He will respond to us as surely as the arrival of dawn or the coming of rains in early spring. HOSEA 6:3

A prayer about the HEART
When I need my heart to be transformed

LORD,

I want to be a woman you can use. Please change my heart! What is keeping me from submitting to your direction? If it is my pride, please help me to develop an attitude of humility. When I humble myself before you, I will be more open to your guidance. I also need to get rid of some sinful habits that are weighing me down and keeping me far from you. Help me to repent, to stop these bad habits, and to choose the righteous way. I know that you want to work in my life to make me more like you. May I practice obeying your Word, and as I do, may I see my heart begin to be transformed into your image.

Throw off your old sinful nature and your former way of life, which is corrupted by lust and deception. Instead, let the Spirit renew your thoughts and attitudes. Put on your new nature, created to be like God—truly righteous and holy.

EPHESIANS 4:22-24

DAY 223 *Prayerful Moment*

✓ A prayer about CHANGE
When I don't see transformation in my life

LORD,
I get discouraged when I don't see a lot of change in my life. I am impatient, but I know that real change doesn't come overnight. You are giving me a new way of thinking. Your process of transformation takes a lifetime, but it is certain—you never fail. I am your work of art in progress! I trust you to work in me at just the right pace.

I am certain that God, who began the good work within you, will continue his work until it is finally finished on the day when Christ Jesus returns. PHILIPPIANS 1:6

DAY 224 *Prayerful Moment*

✓ A prayer about ENCOURAGEMENT
When I need divine encouragement

LORD GOD,
I long for someone to come beside me, to lift me up and strengthen me. I look to others for encouragement, but how much better to receive it from you! Your encouragement inspires me to go on, to renew my commitment and resolve. It gives me hope that my task is not in vain—that I can make a difference. May I always seek courage by looking up to you, the sovereign God.

Be strong and courageous! Do not be afraid or discouraged. For the LORD your God is with you wherever you go.
JOSHUA 1:9

✓ A prayer about EMPTINESS
When my soul is dry and empty

HEAVENLY FATHER,

My heart feels empty today. I feel a loss of motivation, meaning, and purpose, and there seems no reason to go on. I know any of many things can cause this feeling of emptiness—the death of a loved one, the end of a friendship, being ignored or rejected. It's always some sort of loss that empties one's emotional tank. My reserves are used up, Lord, and I have nothing left to give. I'm hungering and thirsting for something to fill me and satisfy me! I know that Satan is always ready to move into my empty heart, wanting to deceive me into thinking that what he offers can satisfy. But I ask for your protection from him. Fill me instead with your love, truth, and goodness through the presence of the Holy Spirit. You are the Living Water that can refresh me eternally. I am waiting on you, Lord, to restore meaning, purpose, and satisfaction in my life.

Jesus stood and shouted to the crowds, "Anyone who is thirsty may come to me! Anyone who believes in me may come and drink! For the Scriptures declare, 'Rivers of living water will flow from his heart.'" JOHN 7:37-38

A prayer about FEARING GOD
When I ponder what it means to fear God

ALMIGHTY GOD,

Jesus called you Abba, or Father, and his sacrifice has given me the right to approach you boldly as my heavenly Father. But you are still the sovereign God of the universe, and so I should also approach you with a huge sense of reverence and awe. You, O Lord, are very great; no one can fathom your greatness! Teach me to have a healthy respect for your power, holiness, and authority, which I think is what the Bible means when it talks about fearing you. Show me that having the right attitude toward you—properly fearing you—is the key to experiencing all your blessings. I know that when I approach you with respect and awe, I will find that you are tender, loving, and compassionate.

What does the LORD your God require of you? He requires only that you fear the LORD your God, and live in a way that pleases him, and love him and serve him with all your heart and soul. And you must always obey the LORD's commands and decrees . . . for your own good.

DEUTERONOMY 10:12-13

✓ A prayer about the PAST

When I wonder how I can live a godly life with sin in my past

DEAR LORD,

My memories of the past are like a photo album that contains snapshots of my life. Some of these snapshots show happy moments, triumphs, family celebrations, or quiet joys. I treasure those. Other snapshots record tragedies, failures, words, or acts that cause me great shame. I would love to lock these away—to tear out the snapshots that expose parts of my life I'd rather forget. Yet your Word tells me that you can redeem my past. I'm encouraged by the example of the apostle Paul, whose memory album must have been full of snapshots from his days of persecuting Christians. He could have carried an immense burden of regret. But you forgave him, and his life became an example of your amazing grace. You gave him the strength to stop wallowing in the past and to look ahead to the glorious promise he had in Christ. May I do the same, Lord. Help me fully accept your forgiveness, and may my past not distract me from the purpose you have for me.

I focus on this one thing: Forgetting the past and looking forward to what lies ahead, I press on to reach the end of the race and receive the heavenly prize for which God, through Christ Jesus, is calling us. PHILIPPIANS 3:13-14

DAY 228

✓ A prayer about HABITS

When I want to make a habit of reading God's Word

HEAVENLY FATHER,

Because of Jesus' teaching, I know that your Word is spiritual food that I need for spiritual life. Your Word provides nourishment for my soul, and I need that nourishment daily. So why do I only read it when I get around to it? I confess my faithlessness in this area. I know that when I don't read the Bible regularly, I drift away from you and lack the right perspective on sin, holiness, and your love. I don't want that, Lord, because when I'm drifting away and when I don't have the right attitude toward sin, I have no chance to experience the mercy and blessings that come from my relationship with you. Draw me close, Lord. Stir up in me the hunger to study your Word and the self-discipline to do it faithfully, knowing that my spiritual well-being depends on it.

The devil came and said to [Jesus], "If you are the Son of God, tell these stones to become loaves of bread." But Jesus told him, "No! The Scriptures say, 'People do not live by bread alone, but by every word that comes from the mouth of God.'" MATTHEW 4:3-4

A prayer about GENEROSITY
When I want to become more generous

LORD,
I want to be generous with my money, and I know that begins not with a dollar amount but with my attitude. How can I be sure that my heart is in the right place? Teach me to observe where my money goes because that will reveal what I care about most. Father, you know that my priorities aren't always right when it comes to money. I'm too concerned with how much I have to spend now and how much I am saving for the future. But those things aren't as important as what I am willing to relinquish. Please develop in me a generous heart that's willing to give. Show me that when I give something that involves sacrifice, my heart will begin changing from stinginess to selflessness. O Lord, you own it all! Everything I have is a gift from you, and only what I invest in your Kingdom will last forever. May that motivate me to share my material possessions freely with your church and with those in need.

Store your treasures in heaven, where moths and rust cannot destroy, and thieves do not break in and steal. Wherever your treasure is, there the desires of your heart will also be.
MATTHEW 6:20-21

DAY 230 *Prayerful Moment*

✓ A prayer about HELP
When I rejoice in God's help

LORD,
I rejoice as I remember the ways you have helped me. You have been faithful to me in the past, and I am confident of your presence and protection in the future. I am amazed that you—who walked with Moses, David, and other saints of the past—are here with me today and tomorrow. You are my help.

I look up to the mountains—does my help come from there? My help comes from the LORD, who made heaven and earth! . . . The LORD keeps watch over you as you come and go, both now and forever. PSALM 121:1-2, 8

DAY 231 *Prayerful Moment*

✓ A prayer about GOD'S PRESENCE
When I want to experience God's presence in my life

LORD GOD,
Often I ask you to be near me. But the truth is that you are omnipresent, so you are already with me at all times. When I feel distance, often I'm the one who has moved away. Please help me to draw near to you. I want to experience closeness with you. Thank you that you have promised in your Word that when I genuinely seek you, I will find you. You are near.

I know the LORD is always with me. I will not be shaken, for he is right beside me. PSALM 16:8

A prayer about JOY

When I long to experience more joy

LORD GOD,

I spend a lot of energy trying to find joy, but I know that what I find in happy events is only temporary. Whether my happiness comes from a beautiful day at the park, a loving conversation with my children, or a delicious meal, the event ends and then I need to find something else to keep myself upbeat. It can be exhausting. But your Word tells me that *you* are the source of the joy that lasts forever. Teach me to follow you and adopt your attitudes so I'll be able to experience inner joy regardless of my circumstances. I know that no matter what happens, you offer hope. You don't promise constant happiness; in fact, Jesus told his disciples that they would have trouble in the world. But you do promise lasting joy for me if I faithfully follow you. That's what I want, Lord. Thank you for the temporary happiness that comes my way, and may I rest in the eternal joy you set before me.

You will show me the way of life, granting me the joy of your presence and the pleasures of living with you forever.
PSALM 16:11

A prayer about PATIENCE
When I need to develop patience

LORD,

I tend to think that patience is a personality trait—something each person either has or lacks. But I'm beginning to learn that patience is a by-product of your presence and work in the human heart. Please help me to understand that it's not something I can achieve all at once; it comes through perseverance and endurance. The most difficult circumstances may be the very ones that stretch my patience and enable it to grow. I encounter frustrating situations every day with my family, my neighbors, or my coworkers, and I want to be able to respond to them with grace and self-control. I know that will come as my patience increases. Encourage me as I take small, faithful steps day by day to cultivate patience. As I do that, I will become more like you.

Put on your new nature, and be renewed as you learn to know your Creator and become like him. . . . Since God chose you to be the holy people he loves, you must clothe yourselves with tenderhearted mercy, kindness, humility, gentleness, and patience. COLOSSIANS 3:10, 12

A prayer about LETTING GO

When I need to give my problems to God

O LORD,

My heart breaks when I think about the story in Exodus 1–2 of Moses' mother, who raised him in the shadow of Pharaoh's decree that all male Hebrew children should die. She cared for her son as long as she could, but then she had to let him go—literally, as she placed him in a basket on the river—entrusting him to your care. I'm clinging so hard to things in my own life, and I wonder how to find the courage to let go. Help me to recognize that when situations are beyond my control, I need to do what is right for as long as I can, and then trust you to take it from there. The more I try to control a situation, the less I hold on to you. That's not what I want, Lord. Please give me the faith to be obedient and to wait for you to work. Teach me that letting go doesn't mean giving up; it means that I'm watching for your next move. May I remember Moses' mother, who entrusted her son to you and then received him back in a way she never could have imagined. You know best and you care about me, so I place this situation in your loving, capable hands.

We put our hope in the LORD. He is our help and our shield. In him our hearts rejoice, for we trust in his holy name. Let your unfailing love surround us, LORD, for our hope is in you alone. PSALM 33:20-22

A prayer about MERCY

When I am aware of God's mercy in my life

MERCIFUL GOD,

You shower amazing kindness on me by not treating me as my sins deserve. At times I have ignored you, neglected you, and rebelled against you, yet in your greatest act of mercy you offer me salvation and eternal life! When you forgive me, your mercy sets me free from the power of sin so that I can choose each day to fight my sinful nature. Your mercy has transformed my life, showing me what it feels like to be loved even when I have not loved in return. O Lord, may this great mercy from you cause an outpouring of love in my heart. I want to be an example of your mercy to others today.

The LORD is compassionate and merciful, slow to get angry and filled with unfailing love. He will not constantly accuse us, nor remain angry forever. He does not punish us for all our sins; he does not deal harshly with us, as we deserve.
PSALM 103:8-10

A prayer about PRAISE

When I want praise to become my natural response to God's presence

O LORD MY GOD,

No human being can come close to comprehending your greatness. Your thoughts are far above my thoughts, and your ways are far above my ways. You are majestic and marvelous, and my natural response is praise. Just as people may burst into applause or cheers when a head of state or a celebrity enters a room, may my natural response when I enter your presence in worship be praise. Your Word tells me that you created the universe, yet you also provide for my needs. You are all-powerful and all-knowing, yet you also care about the details of my life. You alone are worthy of my highest praise! Indeed, when I consider who you are and all you have done for me, praise is my only possible response.

Let all that I am praise the LORD; with my whole heart, I will praise his holy name. Let all that I am praise the LORD; may I never forget the good things he does for me. He forgives all my sins and heals all my diseases. He redeems me from death and crowns me with love and tender mercies. He fills my life with good things. My youth is renewed like the eagle's!

PSALM 103:1-5

DAY 237 *Prayerful Moment*

A prayer about SPIRITUAL GROWTH

When I want to celebrate my deepening relationship with God

LOVING FATHER,

My relationship with you is my source of strength in every situation, and your love and care for me warm my soul and give me hope. You are the author of life, strength, and hope. Thank you for all that you give me. As I continue to grow in my faith, may I reflect your brilliant glory more and more.

Commit everything you do to the LORD. Trust him, and he will help you. He will make your innocence radiate like the dawn, and the justice of your cause will shine like the noonday sun. PSALM 37:5-6

DAY 238 *Prayerful Moment*

A prayer about OBEDIENCE

When gratitude prompts me to obey God

HEAVENLY FATHER,

I have experienced your love and work in my life, and my heart overflows with gratitude. I want to show my appreciation by obeying your commands. Teach me to express my love for you by following your way completely. May my desire to obey and please you grow day by day.

[Jesus said,] "If you love me, obey my commandments."
JOHN 14:15

DAY 239

A prayer about DENIAL
When I wonder what it means to deny myself

LORD,
When I decided to follow you, I made a choice not to base my life on my own will and desires. You call me to deny my self-centered attitudes for the sake of obeying you, to exercise restraint and self-discipline. I want to follow you wholeheartedly, Lord. I love you, and I want to be willing to give up anything you ask if it will draw me closer to you. I am not a finished product yet, but I invite you to work in my heart to accomplish this. I know you will be faithful to finish the work you started in me.

Then Jesus said to his disciples, "If any of you wants to be my follower, you must turn from your selfish ways, take up your cross, and follow me. If you try to hang on to your life, you will lose it. But if you give up your life for my sake, you will save it." MATTHEW 16:24-25

✓ A prayer about DISAPPOINTMENT
When I'm struggling to handle disappointment

HEAVENLY FATHER,

I face disappointment almost every day. It can be because I didn't accomplish everything I hoped to, because someone hurt me, because I let another person down, or because things just didn't go my way. Often I experience that awful feeling of not being good enough, and then I make things worse by blaming others or asking "what if" questions, which lead to regret. I hate this cycle, Lord. It leads only to discouragement, depression, anger, shame, or bitterness. I don't want disappointment to dominate my thoughts. I need you to transform my attitude and renew my perspective. Show me how to view disappointment as an opportunity to learn and grow. Help me to focus on what I have, not on what I've missed. You have promised me a wonderful future, and I know you want me to dwell on what is still ahead, not on what could have been. The next time I feel disappointed, may I remember all you have blessed me with, determine to grow through the experience, and be happy that I have your approval. You're the only one who really matters.

Always continue to fear the LORD. You will be rewarded for this; your hope will not be disappointed.
PROVERBS 23:17-18

✓ ## A prayer about CHOICES
When I need to make better choices

LORD JESUS,
When I look back on my life—or even just on the past few weeks—I can see that I haven't always made the best choices. At times I've chosen to remain in sin, I've purposely walked away from you, and I've pursued paths that were selfish or unwise. But I know choices reflect the kind of woman I am, so I want to choose better. I'm encouraged by the example of Zacchaeus, who certainly made a lot of bad choices by stealing money in his career as a tax collector. But you called him, spent time with him, forgave him—and he was changed. You transformed both his behavior and his attitudes. O Lord, do the same for me, I pray! May I spend more time with you and allow your goodness to permeate my heart. Only then will I begin making choices that please you and avoiding choices that don't. I praise you for your transforming power in my life.

When Jesus came by, he looked up at Zacchaeus and called him by name. "Zacchaeus!" he said. "Quick, come down! I must be a guest in your home today." Zacchaeus quickly climbed down and took Jesus to his house in great excitement and joy. . . . Zacchaeus stood before the Lord and said, "I will give half my wealth to the poor, Lord, and if I have cheated people on their taxes, I will give them back four times as much!" LUKE 19:5-6, 8

A prayer about UNITY

When I'm struggling with lack of Christian unity

HEAVENLY FATHER,

Often I'm convinced that my opinion is the best. So if someone else's opinion is different, I'm sure it must not be right or well thought through. Forgive my arrogance, Lord. I know my mind-set keeps me from listening to new ideas that might actually change my opinion for the better. And when your children hold tight to their own opinions, your church suffers. Give me the humility to realize that I don't have to be right, the wisdom to recognize that others' opinions are just as valid as mine, and the grace to open my ears and listen. Just as different colors create a richer painting, so in your hands, differences among people can create a richer whole. Show me how to celebrate the differences I see in my family and in other believers. As I appreciate those differences, teach me how to fit them together to accomplish a oneness that glorifies you. Then I will experience the true unity you designed humans to share and enjoy.

You are all children of God through faith in Christ Jesus. And all who have been united with Christ in baptism have put on Christ, like putting on new clothes. There is no longer Jew or Gentile, slave or free, male and female. For you are all one in Christ Jesus. GALATIANS 3:26-28

A prayer about LOVE

When I want to learn what it means to love my neighbor

LORD JESUS,

You tell me through your Word, in Luke 10:27, that the greatest commandment is to love you with all my heart, soul, mind, and strength. The second greatest is to love my neighbor as myself. That command shows how well you know me. You know that my first instinct is always to take care of myself. Meeting others' needs in the same way I meet my own is a radical change in thinking, and to do it I have to combat my natural instincts. I can't do that on my own. I need your transforming power to help me care deeply for others. May I remember that every time I show love to others, I am fulfilling your command and demonstrating your compassion.

[Jesus said,] "I am giving you a new commandment: Love each other. Just as I have loved you, you should love each other. Your love for one another will prove to the world that you are my disciples." JOHN 13:34-35

DAY 244 *Prayerful Moment*

✓ A prayer about FAMILY

When I wonder how my family can make a difference

FATHER GOD,

So often I think about my life in individualistic terms: How can *I* make an impact? What can *I* do? But you work through groups of people, too, including families. Show my family how we can influence others for you, Lord. Teach us to serve together, and use us to accomplish great things for your Kingdom.

How joyful are those who fear the LORD and delight in obeying his commands. Their children will be successful everywhere; an entire generation of godly people will be blessed. . . . Their good deeds will last forever.

PSALM 112:1-3

DAY 245 *Prayerful Moment*

✓ A prayer about TRANSFORMATION

When I want to become like Christ

HEAVENLY FATHER,

You are righteous, loving, and just. How can I ever become like you? But your Word tells me that when I believe in you and obey you, your Holy Spirit works in me to change my interests and desires to reflect yours. Thank you for your transforming power in my life.

The Lord—who is the Spirit—makes us more and more like him as we are changed into his glorious image.

2 CORINTHIANS 3:18

✓ A prayer about SORROW
When I wonder if joy will ever overcome my sorrow

LOVING GOD,
Struggle and tears are so often part of my life. Tragedy strikes, losses occur, and I am left sorrowing. I know that you never promised that my faith would keep me from going through difficult times, but you have promised to be with me always. Help me, Lord, to walk through my own "Valley of Weeping" hand in hand with you, growing stronger along the way. May I walk toward you and never turn away, because you alone can redeem my losses with your promises of comfort and hope. I can take heart knowing that grief will not have the last word. You will relieve my sorrow and one day replace it with joy that lasts forever.

What joy for those whose strength comes from the LORD, who have set their minds on a pilgrimage to Jerusalem. When they walk through the Valley of Weeping, it will become a place of refreshing springs. The autumn rains will clothe it with blessings. They will continue to grow stronger, and each of them will appear before God in Jerusalem.
PSALM 84:5-7

DAY 247

A prayer about ABSOLUTES
When I ponder God's absolutes

FATHER GOD,

Your Word is my instruction book; it's a manual that tells me how to get the most out of my life. Sometimes I prefer to go my own way, but I know you have programmed certain absolutes into the world. They apply to all people, in all times, and in all places. Teach me, Lord, that when I ignore your instructions, I'll miss much of what you intend for me to enjoy. Even worse, when I go against your instructions, I often end up hurt, frustrated, and disappointed. Impress on me the importance of reading your Word, discovering your absolutes, and living by them. Only then will I find fulfillment in my life.

All Scripture is inspired by God and is useful to teach us what is true and to make us realize what is wrong in our lives. It corrects us when we are wrong and teaches us to do what is right. God uses it to prepare and equip his people to do every good work. 2 TIMOTHY 3:16-17

A prayer about SPIRITUAL GROWTH
When I'm feeling dry and empty

LORD GOD,

My soul is dry, thirsting for something that will be truly fulfilling. I'm dealing with the heat of temptation and the pressures of life, and that has caused a season of drought in my soul. My desire to know you and serve you just seems to have wilted. Help me, Lord. I need you to revive me. May I not neglect the life-giving source of your Word. As I immerse myself in it, I know it will refresh me, quenching my thirst and bringing new growth. Just as you send the rain to refresh the earth, you also send opportunities that will help revive my passion for you. May I always take these opportunities to move out of the wasteland back to the greener pastures of connection with you. Give me the strength to persevere, Lord, knowing that you will draw me to yourself and restore joy to me.

The LORD will guide you continually, giving you water when you are dry and restoring your strength. You will be like a well-watered garden, like an ever-flowing spring.
ISAIAH 58:11

DAY 249

✓ A prayer about COMPETITION

When competing with others is causing harm

HEAVENLY FATHER,

You have given me a competitive nature. There are times when I want to be the best, to win, to excel. Pursuing excellence is fine, but I run into trouble when my desire to be first means that I view other people solely as my competitors. Never let me forget that they are created in your image, deserving of your love too. May I focus not on being better than others but simply on doing my best. Only then will my efforts honor you. And guard me from allowing my competitive drive to cause me to concentrate too much on my own goals rather than on your plans for me—help me to focus on what you want me to achieve, Lord. Without your guidance, my achievements won't have lasting value. Please channel my competitive nature into the pursuit of accomplishments and actions that will last for eternity.

Whatever I am now, it is all because God poured out his special favor on me—and not without results. For I have worked harder than any of the other apostles; yet it was not I but God who was working through me by his grace.

1 CORINTHIANS 15:10

A prayer about APOLOGY
When I need to make something right

LORD GOD,
Saying that I'm sorry for something I did wrong is difficult for me. My pride so often gets in the way, and I know that can have devastating effects on my life and relationships. Help me, Lord, to be willing to apologize. I know this will open the door to healing and blessing. Teach me to face the issue head-on, admit my fault, and then humble myself enough to confess it to the one I have wronged. May my sincere apology be the first step in changing my behavior and committing to do the right thing from that point on. Thank you that you are always willing to hear my contrite apology and respond with grace and forgiveness.

His son said to him, "Father, I have sinned against both heaven and you, and I am no longer worthy of being called your son." But his father said to the servants, "Quick! Bring the finest robe in the house and put it on him. . . . For this son of mine was dead and has now returned to life. He was lost, but now he is found." LUKE 15:21-22, 24

DAY 251 *Prayerful Moment*

✓ **A prayer about PATIENCE**
When I wonder how waiting can make my faith stronger

LORD,
You often ask me to wait. Sometimes waiting saves me from defeat, and other times it prepares me for a special task you have for me. I may not understand why, Lord, but please teach me that waiting is never time wasted. May I not misuse it by being anxious for whatever is next. I want to serve you even as I wait for you to accomplish the next good thing in my life.

Be still in the presence of the LORD, and wait patiently for him to act. PSALM 37:7

DAY 252 *Prayerful Moment*

✓ **A prayer about GRATITUDE**
When I am thankful for God's blessings

LORD GOD,
You have given me far more than I realize—life, salvation, your Holy Spirit, comfort, encouragement, freedom from sin. And it's all undeserved! You gave it all freely because of your love for me. O Lord, may I never become ungrateful; instead, may I always respond with overflowing thankfulness for your kindness to me.

It is good to give thanks to the LORD . . . to proclaim your unfailing love in the morning, your faithfulness in the evening. PSALM 92:1-2

A prayer about the WILL OF GOD

When I wonder what purpose God has for me

FATHER GOD,

In your Word you have set forth your general will for all people. If I follow your commands with my whole heart, I will stay morally pure, connected with you, and loving toward others. That's certainly your will for me. But I know that you also created me for a specific purpose, and you call me to do certain tasks. When I'm uncertain about what to do, remind me again that it's often through steady obedience to your general will that I find your specific direction. I'm so thankful that you are vitally interested in the details of my life: you care about them, and they matter to you. Yet someday, when I enter into eternity, I know the specifics of what job I took or what house I bought won't be as important as whether I was faithful in loving and serving you. May I make simple obedience my focus today.

Seek his will in all you do, and he will show you which path to take. PROVERBS 3:6

A prayer about SANCTIFICATION
When I need reassurance that God is still working in me

FATHER GOD,

I am clinging to your promise that you will finish what you start. You have saved me, taking me out of my sinfulness and despair and bringing me into relationship with you. Now you are sanctifying me, changing me slowly but surely from the woman I used to be to the woman you created me to be—you have started that process, and you will not stop. I am struggling right now, and I see my shortcomings far more clearly than the change you've effected. I'm well aware of my limitations, but may they never blind me to the promise that you will complete your work in me. I know that you can take my present insecurities and transform them into powerful opportunities to work in my heart. May I be malleable as you shape me, and may I patiently rest in your timing as you guide me to where I need to be.

God is working in you, giving you the desire and the power to do what pleases him. . . . Live clean, innocent lives as children of God, shining like bright lights in a world full of crooked and perverse people. PHILIPPIANS 2:13, 15

DAY 255

A prayer about INSPIRATION

When I hope my choices inspire others to follow God

HEAVENLY FATHER,

You have given me the freedom to make my own choices, and I know it's my responsibility to make the right ones. I choose to stand up for you and your ways! Lord, I want the discipline to be fiercely committed to obeying your Word no matter what. I want the courage to live out the purpose you have for my life, even in the face of danger or ridicule. Give me the steadfastness to choose the right thing and never compromise. May I follow you fearlessly and serve you faithfully, following the example of so many others in your Word. And as I do, may my example inspire others to follow—not because they see me, but because they see you shining through me. Thank you, Father, for the incredible privilege of serving you.

Don't let anyone think less of you because you are young. Be an example to all believers in what you say, in the way you live, in your love, your faith, and your purity.

1 TIMOTHY 4:12

✓ A prayer about DEPRESSION
When I'm experiencing depression

LORD,
I'm struggling with depression. Sometimes it descends slowly and hangs in the air like an all-day rain. Other times it overwhelms me like an avalanche of darkness. I've had it come as the result of a specific painful event, and I've had it come for no discernible reason. I hate the way I feel right now, but I cling to your promise that you have not abandoned me. No matter how low I get, there is no depth I can reach that is too low for you. Even when I don't feel your presence, you are with me. O God, please don't let this pain be wasted. Use it! May it help me to slow down and rest in your presence. As I pray and read your Word, may the Holy Spirit do his work of comfort, transformation, and encouragement. I long for the light of your comforting presence to drive the darkness of depression from my soul.

Jesus said, "Come to me, all of you who are weary and carry heavy burdens, and I will give you rest."
MATTHEW 11:28

A prayer about MIRACLES
When I wonder whether miracles still happen

GOD,

Sometimes the miracles I read about in the Bible seem like ancient myths. But just as Pharaoh was blind to the miracles you performed right before his eyes, I know I am sometimes blind to the mighty work you are doing around me. I think of miracles as dramatic events, such as raising a dead person to life, but they're not always so obvious. Unveil my eyes so I can see your intervention in my life and the miracles happening all around me. The birth of a baby, an amazing sunset, the healing of an illness, the restoration of a seemingly hopeless relationship, the rebirth of the earth in the spring, the wonder of salvation by faith alone, and your specific call on my life are just a few. May I have the faith to see that you are constantly at work in the world, in beautiful and powerful ways.

Come and see what our God has done, what awesome miracles he performs for people! PSALM 66:5

DAY 258 *Prayerful Moment*

✓ **A prayer about WORK**
When I'm not sure my work has purpose

LORD GOD,
You have called me to work diligently and with enthusiasm at whatever I do, whether I'm a mom at home raising my children or a professional working at a salaried job. Train me to think of my daily tasks as having been assigned by you. With that perspective, I will feel more purposeful, and I will begin to work for your approval instead of anyone else's. May I always work enthusiastically for you so that I can be proud of the work I do.

Never be lazy, but work hard and serve the Lord enthusiastically. ROMANS 12:11

DAY 259 *Prayerful Moment*

✓ **A prayer about being an EXAMPLE**
When I want to be an example to those around me

HEAVENLY FATHER,
I want to be a role model for those around me. Whether it's my family members, coworkers, or friends, I need your help to be a godly influence. Teach me to have a servant's heart, to take responsibility for my actions, and to refuse to stay silent when something is unjust. May I live with kindness, integrity, and deep love for you, always being mindful of the example I am setting.

Let your good deeds shine out for all to see, so that everyone will praise your heavenly Father. MATTHEW 5:16

A prayer about FAILURE
When I wonder how God defines failure

HOLY GOD,
So many voices in my culture tell me that success involves things such as having a high-powered job, raising a perfect family, winning all kinds of community awards, and retiring comfortably. But if I did all these things apart from you, you would still say that I had failed. Failure in your eyes is when I am not living the way you created me to live. And you gave me the gift of life and created me for relationship with you—so my greatest failure would be to reject that. May I never fail by neglecting or ignoring you. May I acknowledge my need for you and live your perfect plan for my life.

[Jesus said,] "Anyone who listens to my teaching and follows it is wise, like a person who builds a house on solid rock. Though the rain comes in torrents and the floodwaters rise and the winds beat against that house, it won't collapse because it is built on bedrock. But anyone who hears my teaching and doesn't obey it is foolish, like a person who builds a house on sand. When the rains and floods come and the winds beat against that house, it will collapse with a mighty crash." MATTHEW 7:24-27

A prayer when I experience LONELINESS
When I feel as if God is absent

LORD GOD,

The greater my troubles, the further away you sometimes seem. In my darkest hours, I'm afraid that you have left me all alone. But in times like these, teach me not to trust my feelings. Help me instead to trust your promise that you will never leave me—I need to rely on what your Word tells me is true. You are near, alongside me. After all, one of your names is Immanuel, God with us! O Lord, thank you that when I am hurting the most, you understand and will ease my pain. Even in my loneliest moments, I find peace and comfort in your presence.

You know when I sit down or stand up. You know my thoughts even when I'm far away. You see me when I travel and when I rest at home. You know everything I do. You know what I am going to say even before I say it, LORD. You go before me and follow me. You place your hand of blessing on my head. PSALM 139:2-5

A prayer about EXCELLENCE

When I need to strive to do my best

LORD JESUS,

You set the standard for excellence. Your creation is marvelously complex and amazingly beautiful. No artist could ever paint a picture that rivals one of your real-life sunsets! You initiated excellence, and you call me to pursue it in my own life. When I do, may others get a glimpse of your character and be inspired to pursue excellence themselves. If ever I'm unsure what excellence looks like in this life, remind me of Hebrews 12:2, which says to fix my eyes on you, the author and perfecter of my faith. May I model myself after you, working to reflect your character and accomplish your will. When I do shoddy work, it's often because I feel apathetic. Teach me always to do my best with the tasks before me. May I be committed to doing things the right way and helping others to the best of my ability.

By his divine power, God has given us everything we need for living a godly life. We have received all of this by coming to know him, the one who called us to himself by means of his marvelous glory and excellence. 2 PETER 1:3

A prayer about COMPROMISE

When is it right to compromise?

HEAVENLY FATHER,

It's easy to see in children, especially when they are in conflict with one another, the kind of stubbornness that avoids compromise. Both sides want their way, and neither wants to give in. But I'm afraid I can see myself in that scenario too. Forgive me for the times when I'm so inflexible that I refuse to give ground to someone else. For the sake of harmony in my relationships, teach me the art of compromise—looking beyond my desires to the greater good and negotiating so that both sides win. But keep me alert, Lord, to the times when I must not compromise. May I never give in when I'm tempted to sin or to compromise your truth, your ways, or your Word. Guard me from giving up godliness in exchange for anything else. I know that's never a compromise you want me to make. May I always choose your ways above my own.

Make me truly happy by agreeing wholeheartedly with each other, loving one another, and working together with one mind and purpose. PHILIPPIANS 2:2

A prayer about TIME
When I need help managing my time

LORD GOD,
I never feel as if I have enough time to do the things I need to do. I'm pulled in so many directions—home, family, job, volunteer work, church—and it's hard for me to prioritize. I feel overwhelmed, and I need your help! Only you can set my priorities straight. Teach me that the best way to find the time I need is to devote more time to you. Only then will I know more clearly what you want me to do; only then will I understand your priorities for me. O Lord, just as you commanded the Israelites to set aside the Sabbath for rest, you ask me to set aside time for you. May I never look on this as a burden but as your way of freeing me from the exhaustion that comes from my constant striving to do everything I feel I need to do. As I rest in you, clear my vision and help me to focus on what is important to you. Then everything else will fall in place.

Remember to observe the Sabbath day by keeping it holy. You have six days each week for your ordinary work, but the seventh day is a Sabbath day of rest dedicated to the LORD your God. . . . For in six days the LORD made the heavens, the earth, the sea, and everything in them; but on the seventh day he rested. That is why the LORD blessed the Sabbath day and set it apart as holy. EXODUS 20:8-11

DAY 265 *Prayerful Moment*

✓ A prayer about FAITH
When I want to affirm my trust in God

HEAVENLY FATHER,
Faith is more than just believing; it is entrusting my very life to what I believe. I trust you with my whole life, Lord. May I always be willing to follow your guidelines for living, because I am convinced that your way is the best for me. You are God, and I believe you will keep your promises about salvation and eternal life. I place my faith completely in you.

Faith is the confidence that what we hope for will actually happen; it gives us assurance about things we cannot see.
HEBREWS 11:1

DAY 266 *Prayerful Moment*

✓ A prayer about DEPENDENCE
When I need to acknowledge my dependence on God

HEAVENLY FATHER,
Sometimes I strive to be self-sufficient, but really, why wouldn't I want to depend on you? There's no one more reliable than you are: what you promise will come true. Teach me that the more I humble myself and depend on you, the stronger I become in character and integrity. May I become completely dependent on you so that I will completely rely on your strength.

Humble yourselves before the Lord, and he will lift you up in honor. JAMES 4:10

A prayer about BEAUTY
When I want to reflect God's beauty

HEAVENLY FATHER,
Things are loveliest and best when they are blooming at their right time. I know that people have many seasons, too, and beauty changes in each one. The beauty of an older woman is quite different from that of a twenty-year-old, and the appeal of an infant is different from the emerging attractiveness of an adolescent. But the aura that comes from grace, sweetness, and charm flows from one season of life to the next. Lord, I know that those who closely follow you reflect the beauty of your holiness, love, and wisdom. Please keep me from envying those in a different time of life; instead, help me to accept the season in which I'm now living and reflect you to the fullest. As you work in my heart, may I exhibit grace. I want others to see your unfading beauty in me.

Don't be concerned about the outward beauty of fancy hairstyles, expensive jewelry, or beautiful clothes. You should clothe yourselves instead with the beauty that comes from within, the unfading beauty of a gentle and quiet spirit, which is so precious to God. 1 PETER 3:3-4

DAY 268

A prayer about FINISHING

When I need to follow through on what I started

DEAR LORD,

Often I have good intentions, but I don't always follow through on them. Then I'm disappointed that I didn't do something worthwhile. I need your help to develop the self-discipline to finish what I start. I know that having a clear picture of the end goal will help me; when I see where I'm going and what my good intentions can accomplish, I'll be more motivated to follow through. Lord, I want to set goals to make changes in my life—to be healthier, spend more time with my family, read your Word more consistently, and/or find a service opportunity that fits my gifts. Please empower me with the perseverance to follow through until these intentions become a reality. May I finish all the tasks you set before me.

Let us run with endurance the race God has set before us. We do this by keeping our eyes on Jesus, the champion who initiates and perfects our faith. HEBREWS 12:1-2

A prayer about AMBITION
When I need to reevaluate my ambitions

HOLY GOD,

I long to be a part of your great work in the world. But sometimes I think I cross the line into wanting to achieve status through doing your work. I know that's dangerous because that's when I stop thinking about *serving* you and start trying to *use* you. Forgive me, Lord. Help me to take hold of my selfish ambition and keep it from becoming a hook for Satan to tempt me away from you. Remind me of Jesus' example when he was offered worldly power. Give me the wisdom to see when the things I want to do would draw me closer to you and when they would pull me away. Then teach me the self-discipline to make the right choices. May my desires for things in this world never keep me from better things you desire for me.

The devil took [Jesus] to the peak of a very high mountain and showed him all the kingdoms of the world and their glory. "I will give it all to you," he said, "if you will kneel down and worship me." "Get out of here, Satan," Jesus told him. "For the Scriptures say, 'You must worship the L*ORD your God and serve only him.'"* MATTHEW 4:8-10

✓ ## A prayer about GOD'S CARE
When I need reassurance of God's care for me

LOVING GOD,
When I feel frustrated or distressed, I start to doubt your love for me. Do you really care? I turn to your Word and am reassured by the many passages that speak of your deeply personal love. You loved me before I was even born! You created me to have a relationship with you, and you give me the opportunity to live with you and be loved by you forever. In what greater way could you show that you care for me? You know me intimately and treat me as an individual. I'm so grateful that you urge me to bring my needs and worries to you. You care about what happens to me! Thank you that no matter how other people treat me, you can break through my feelings of loneliness and tend to my deepest needs and worries with incredible compassion.

O Lord, you alone are my hope. I've trusted you, O Lord, from childhood. Yes, you have been with me from birth; from my mother's womb you have cared for me. No wonder I am always praising you! PSALM 71:5-6

A prayer about STRENGTH
When I need God's strength

LORD,
In our culture, people seem to equate following you with being weak. That's not true! It's easy to do whatever I feel like doing—that takes no discipline at all. But it takes strength to humbly obey you when I'm tempted to sin, or to humbly serve others when I don't feel like it. I don't always have that resolve, Lord. Often I struggle with sin, and then I'm overwhelmed by my weakness and doubt whether I could do anything worthwhile for you. At those times I take comfort in the fact that your wisdom and power are demonstrated even better through my weaknesses than through my strengths. When I depend on my willpower, I am weak and I will fail. When I allow you to work through my weaknesses, I am strong. Only then can I be used by you to demonstrate your love and power. Teach me always to depend on your strength, not my own.

I take pleasure in my weaknesses, and in the insults, hardships, persecutions, and troubles that I suffer for Christ. For when I am weak, then I am strong.
2 CORINTHIANS 12:10

DAY 272 *Prayerful Moment*

A prayer about FREEDOM
When I consider what true freedom is

LOVING GOD,
You created humans with the freedom to love you, obey you, and do what is right—or to turn away from you and do what is wrong. You gave me this freedom because you don't want to force me to yourself through coercion; you want me to respond willingly out of gratitude for the love you have shown me. Thank you for the ultimate freedom I find when I come to you.

You have been called to live in freedom. GALATIANS 5:13

DAY 273 *Prayerful Moment*

A prayer about DISCOURAGEMENT
When discouragement has sapped my motivation

DEAR LORD,
I'm discouraged right now, and that discouragement has drained my energy and confidence. Even when outward circumstances threaten to crush me, Lord, please sustain me by giving me a strong sense of your presence, your call on my life, and your love for me. As I focus on these things, renew my sense of purpose and help me to move forward. Wipe away this discouragement and empower me to follow you with enthusiasm.

Since God in his mercy has given us this new way, we never give up. . . . For our present troubles are small and won't last very long. 2 CORINTHIANS 4:1, 17

A prayer about INTIMACY

When I want to cultivate intimate relationships

LORD,

I long to be connected with others—heart to heart, mind to mind, and soul to soul. You have created me to desire intimate relationships where I can share my burdens, fears, and joys and help others bear their burdens as well. These heart-level connections will ease my loneliness, make me feel known, and increase my compassion for others. But the most profound kind of intimacy is intimacy with you. Your Word calls the church your bride! You reveal yourself to me and allow me to learn about your heart. You are the source of love, and you have created me with the ability to love. When I experience intimacy with you, I feel your love to the fullest and return that love to you. What a gift! Knowing you not only changes me, but gives all my other relationships new and greater meaning.

"When that day comes," says the LORD, "you will call me 'my husband' instead of 'my master.' . . . I will make you my wife forever, showing you righteousness and justice, unfailing love and compassion. I will be faithful to you and make you mine, and you will finally know me as the LORD."

HOSEA 2:16, 19-20

✓ A prayer about SECURITY
When I'm looking in the Bible for security

FATHER GOD,
In this ever-changing world, only a few things are certain. You have given me an incredible gift in the changeless truths I find in the Bible. No matter what else fails, I know that when I follow the commands in your Word, I can have the assurance that I am doing the right thing. The fundamental principles of right and wrong, true and false, good and bad never change because you established them at the creation of the universe. Help me take time to meditate on Scripture, commit verses to memory, and build my faith day by day on the truths I find in your Word. Then I will have a solid foundation that will not easily crack under the world's pressure.

The instructions of the LORD are perfect, reviving the soul. The decrees of the LORD are trustworthy, making wise the simple. The commandments of the LORD are right, bringing joy to the heart. The commands of the LORD are clear, giving insight for living. PSALM 19:7-8

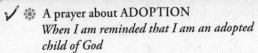

✓ A prayer about ADOPTION
When I am reminded that I am an adopted child of God

DEAR LORD,
Thank you for adoption, which is a beautiful example of your love for me. Just as adoptive parents make a choice to give a child a new life, so you chose to give me a new life in you that I could not achieve on my own. People who adopt children decide to lovingly teach and nurture them and give them the rights and privileges that come with being a member of their family. You have done the same for me, and I praise you! I am privileged to receive all your blessings, both in this life and the next.

Even before he made the world, God loved us and chose us in Christ to be holy and without fault in his eyes. God decided in advance to adopt us into his own family by bringing us to himself through Jesus Christ. This is what he wanted to do, and it gave him great pleasure. So we praise God for the glorious grace he has poured out on us who belong to his dear Son.
EPHESIANS 1:4-6

A prayer about THOUGHTS

When I wonder whether my thoughts matter

LORD GOD,

I try to be careful about what I do, because I want to please you and because I want to be a good witness to others. I have to admit that I'm much less careful about what I think. No one can see or hear my thoughts, after all. Do they really matter? But your Word tells me that what is in my mind is crucial because it's in my thoughts that actions and words have their beginning. Forgive me, Lord, for letting my thoughts have free rein. Please give me the self-discipline to stop thinking about things that are ungodly. Control my heart, Lord, and inspire my mind to produce godly thoughts, which will in turn produce godly actions.

It is what comes from inside that defiles you. For from within, out of a person's heart, come evil thoughts, sexual immorality, theft, murder, adultery, greed, wickedness, deceit, lustful desires, envy, slander, pride, and foolishness.

MARK 7:20-22

DAY 278

A prayer about GOD'S HAND
When I am amazed that God would pursue me

ALMIGHTY GOD,
I am amazed when I read in your Word that you are looking for a personal relationship with each person you have created—including me! I am a sinner, yet you pursue me. You do it not to get something from me but to give wonderful things to me: help, hope, power, salvation, joy, peace, eternal life. You pursue me because you love me, and you know how these gifts can transform my life forever. I'm grateful that, because you want the best for me, you relentlessly call me to turn away from sin and turn to an eternal relationship with you. Your desire is that no one would reject you, yet you allow each person the freedom to return your love or to spend eternity apart from you. Thank you, Lord, for pursuing me even in my unworthiness. You call me your child, and I am overcome with awe and gratitude. May I always be captivated by your pursuing, unfailing love.

Surely your goodness and unfailing love will pursue me all the days of my life, and I will live in the house of the LORD *forever.* PSALM 23:6

DAY 279 *Prayerful Moment*

✓ A prayer about FAITHFULNESS
When I need to be careful of falling into sin

LORD,
I don't want to fall into sin, so I know I need to guard my heart. Teach me to stop problems before they start by guarding my heart from ungodly thinking. I can't trust my emotions to tell me what is right or good because they're too easily swayed. Instead, may I always trust your Word to guide me. The truths there come from your heart, which is good and perfect.

Guard your heart above all else, for it determines the course of your life. PROVERBS 4:23

DAY 280 *Prayerful Moment*

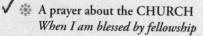

✓ A prayer about the CHURCH
When I am blessed by fellowship

LORD,
All my good friends are wonderful gifts. But the fellowship I experience at church among other believers is unique because you, almighty God, are present there. Thank you for fellowship where I can share honestly about the things that really matter, receive encouragement to stay strong in the face of temptation and persecution, and hear your wisdom for dealing with problems.

Let us not neglect our meeting together, as some people do, but encourage one another, especially now that the day of his return is drawing near. HEBREWS 10:25

A prayer about PASSION

When I want to be fully committed to God

HEAVENLY FATHER,

Relationships with parents, husbands, children, and friends take effort and energy. My relationship with you is no exception. Thank you that you are faithful; you remain fully committed to me even when my commitment to you wavers. Help me, Lord, to be diligent in my efforts to know you better—that's what will make our relationship deeper and more exciting. May I consistently study your Word, which will help me understand your heart and hear your voice. May I have a thankful heart, which will cause me to see your goodness and blessings everywhere I look. And may I serve others, which will require me to take my eyes off myself and experience the excitement of being part of your purpose. Please take the embers of my passion for you and blow them into a flame!

I will give them singleness of heart and put a new spirit within them. I will take away their stony, stubborn heart and give them a tender, responsive heart. EZEKIEL 11:19

✓ ## A prayer about CONSCIENCE
When I want a clear conscience

LORD GOD,

You alone know my heart. I can fool others by acting good and by looking good on the outside, but I can't fool you. You see my thoughts, my attitudes, and my motives. You're far more concerned about the condition of my heart than about my external behavior because actions always flow from the heart. Sometimes I want to hide from you, but give me the courage to lay myself bare before you and welcome your examination. Show me the selfishness and impurity that are present in me, and root them out before they affect my actions. I know I need your cleansing. Then I'll be able to say that my conscience is clear and my heart will be open to you as you work in me and through me.

How can I know all the sins lurking in my heart? Cleanse me from these hidden faults. Keep your servant from deliberate sins! Don't let them control me. Then I will be free of guilt and innocent of great sin. May the words of my mouth and the meditation of my heart be pleasing to you, O LORD, my rock and my redeemer. PSALM 19:12-14

DAY 283

A prayer about EMPATHY

When I want to grow in empathy

HEAVENLY FATHER,

It's usually not difficult for me to feel bad for someone who is going through a hard time or to feel glad for someone who has had success. That kind of quick sympathy doesn't cost much. But I want to be deeper than that. I want to experience empathy—to feel the same emotions that other people feel. When I have empathy, there won't be room to feel jealousy over a friend's success or to enjoy the failure of an enemy. Lord, as I pursue this kind of compassion, I know you can break through to my heart, softening it toward others and helping me know how to comfort them, support them, and meet their needs. As I seek to understand people, may I grow in my knowledge of how best to show love to them in obedience to your commandment to love one another.

Be happy with those who are happy, and weep with those who weep. ROMANS 12:15

✓ A prayer about KINDNESS
When I ponder the meaning of kindness

LOVING GOD,

You call me to love others and be kind; in fact, 1 Corinthians 13:4 says that love is kind. But I think sometimes I mistake being "nice" for being kind—being nice involves surface politeness, but you call me to something much deeper and more proactive. As I strive to be kind, teach me to generously share what I have with others and help those in need, even when I don't know them. Show me how to look for opportunities to help when others are in trouble. Empower me to show forgiveness and mercy to people, though there may be times when they don't deserve it. Train me to use encouraging, helpful words instead of criticizing others. Being nice is about keeping the peace, but being kind means I may need to confront others or teach them to be peace loving and patient. This is so much more than I can do in my own strength, God, but I know that you will help me. May I begin to show kindness in the small things I do and say until it becomes a habit even in the big things. Thank you that you see and reward every act of kindness, no matter how small.

[Jesus said,] "If you give even a cup of cold water to one of the least of my followers, you will surely be rewarded."
MATTHEW 10:42

DAY 285

A prayer about SECURITY

When I consider how knowing God gives me true security

LORD JESUS,

I admit that my security is important to me. Whether it's building up retirement savings, driving a reliable vehicle, living in a safe neighborhood, or keeping supplies on hand for emergencies, I always try to be prepared. But the reality of this life is that sooner or later, my security—whether it's financial, personal, relational, occupational, or even national—will be threatened. The world is constantly changing, and I have learned the hard way that nothing in this world is genuinely secure. Teach me not to grasp so tightly those things that will not last. Instead, remind me of the only things in which I can truly find security: you and your Word. The greatest gift you have given me is eternal security: I know that my future is secure in heaven because I have trusted you as my Savior. What more do I need?

If you confess with your mouth that Jesus is Lord and believe in your heart that God raised him from the dead, you will be saved. ROMANS 10:9

DAY 286 *Prayerful Moment*

✓ A prayer about MOTIVATION
When I'm motivated by joy

HEAVENLY FATHER,
Following you is serious; it's the most important thing in my life. I also find great delight in knowing that you, the God of the universe, love me and have a plan to use me in in your service. Your Word tells me to serve you enthusiastically and joyfully. These positive emotions inspire me to serve you. Thank you for the great motivation I experience when my actions are compelled by love and joy.

Don't be dejected and sad, for the joy of the LORD is your strength! NEHEMIAH 8:10

DAY 287 *Prayerful Moment*

✓ A prayer about FAITHFULNESS
When I want to celebrate God's faithfulness to me

LORD GOD,
You faithfully do what you say you will do. As I read the Bible, I discover myriads of promises you have already fulfilled—so when I read about promises yet to come, I can count on you to keep them. I praise you for listening to those you love, including me. You may not answer in the way I expect, but you faithfully respond. Thank you for your constant love.

God . . . is faithful to do what he says, and he has invited you into partnership with his Son, Jesus Christ our Lord. 1 CORINTHIANS 1:9

A prayer about CONFORMITY
When the world is trying to fit me into its mold

DEAR LORD,
Too often I feel that society is trying to mold me into its way of looking, thinking, and behaving, just like a potter shapes a lump of clay into whatever design the potter has planned. But my culture rarely values what you do, so I need to resist its mold. You have called me to be countercultural. I have to break away from society's rules—but not to go my own way. Instead, I need to conform to your way of thinking and acting, even when it goes against what's popular. I confess that this can be difficult for me, but I want to do it because I want to act as your representative. I want my actions to be consistent with my faith so that others will see your life-changing power in me. You are the Potter, Lord. Reshape me so that I conform to your ways. May my example be a testimony to your grace and power.

Don't copy the behavior and customs of this world, but let God transform you into a new person by changing the way you think. Then you will learn to know God's will for you, which is good and pleasing and perfect. ROMANS 12:2

A prayer about PRAYER

When I want to draw closer to God through prayer

HEAVENLY FATHER,

I long to know you more, and I know that having consistent times of prayer is one of the best ways to grow more intimately connected with you. Sometimes praying feels awkward to me, but I need to remember that it's just talking to you. As I talk, Lord, may I praise you and thank you, confess my sins, make requests, express my pain and frustration, and share what is happening in my life. Cause me also to be still in times of prayer so that I may learn to listen. When I am in tune with your voice, I know that you will make your wisdom and resources available to me. You promise in your Word that you will give good gifts to those who ask you!

[Jesus said,] "Keep on asking, and you will receive what you ask for. Keep on seeking, and you will find. Keep on knocking, and the door will be opened to you. For everyone who asks, receives. Everyone who seeks, finds. And to everyone who knocks, the door will be opened. You parents—if your children ask for a loaf of bread, do you give them a stone instead? Or if they ask for a fish, do you give them a snake? Of course not! So if you sinful people know how to give good gifts to your children, how much more will your heavenly Father give good gifts to those who ask him."

MATTHEW 7:7-11

A prayer about HAPPINESS
When I wonder how I can find happiness

LOVING GOD,
It's part of human nature to desire happiness, but people pursue it in very different ways. I see people around me who bring unhappiness on themselves by choosing destructive lifestyles, and I confess that sometimes I do that myself. If I crave acceptance, I may be tempted to choose sexual involvement outside of marriage, which will lead to pain and emotional scars. If I believe I can find happiness through wealth, I might be tempted to use dishonest means to acquire riches. Guard me from settling for these human counterfeits! Impress on my heart that true, lasting happiness comes by following the principles you designed for my long-term well-being. You graciously provide positive, beautiful life principles throughout your Word. By doing what is right, I'll be able to enjoy life without fear of how my life might turn out. May I always obey your Word, and in doing that, may I find the true happiness that comes from you.

Joyful are people of integrity, who follow the instructions of the LORD. Joyful are those who obey his laws and search for him with all their hearts. They do not compromise with evil, and they walk only in his paths. PSALM 119:1-3

A prayer about DOUBT

When I wonder whether God can use me

ALMIGHTY GOD,

When you came to Moses and called him to lead your people out of Egypt, he was sure he could not do what you were asking of him. The task was too big, and he was scared, unprepared, and full of doubt. But in some ways this was his greatest asset! Your Word tells me that you work through humble hearts that depend on you. When I know I can't do the job through my own power or skill, I have two choices: walk away or let you work through me. O Lord, sometimes the task ahead of me seems so big, and I doubt my ability to persevere. But when I know you want me to keep on going, I must trust you to be faithful to fulfill your purposes.

Moses pleaded with the LORD, "O Lord, I'm not very good with words. I never have been, and I'm not now, even though you have spoken to me. I get tongue-tied, and my words get tangled." Then the LORD asked Moses, "Who makes a person's mouth? Who decides whether people speak or do not speak, hear or do not hear, see or do not see? Is it not I, the LORD? Now go! I will be with you as you speak, and I will instruct you in what to say." EXODUS 4:10-12

A prayer about COURAGE
When I need courage in the face of difficulty

LORD GOD,
I wish scary situations never came up in my life, but they do. Extreme stress, major illness, financial difficulties, and strained family relationships are just a few I've faced. When I'm encountering situations like these, I don't feel very brave. Help me to remember that I don't have to be strong by myself. True courage comes from understanding that you are stronger than my biggest problem or my worst enemy. Your Word makes clear that you want to help me by giving me your power! Thank you, Lord, that even when my faith is shaky, I can have absolute confidence in your strength. I am afraid when I feel as if I am facing a great threat alone. But when I know you are beside me helping me fight the threat, I can be courageous. May I never forget your presence with me. Build up my courage so I may be able to face whatever lies ahead.

Don't be afraid, for I am with you. Don't be discouraged, for I am your God. I will strengthen you and help you. I will hold you up with my victorious right hand.
ISAIAH 41:10

DAY 293 *Prayerful Moment*

✓ A prayer about ENDURANCE

When I'm tempted to give up

LORD GOD,

I am at the end of my strength. My only hope is to depend on your strength to endure. You sustain me, giving me energy to keep going when I am exhausted and faith to keep believing when I am discouraged. Like the fire that purifies precious metals and hardens fine pottery, may my endurance through trials solidify my faith, bringing glory to you.

These trials will show that your faith is genuine. It is being tested as fire tests and purifies gold—though your faith is far more precious than mere gold. 1 PETER 1:7

DAY 294 *Prayerful Moment*

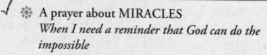

✓ A prayer about MIRACLES

When I need a reminder that God can do the impossible

ALMIGHTY GOD,

You spoke all creation into existence. You are sovereign over all. And you specialize in doing what from a human perspective seems impossible. When I am faced with a problem that seems insurmountable, may I never forget that everything is possible for you. Without fail, you will accomplish your plans for this world—and for my life.

I will boast only in the LORD; let all who are helpless take heart. Come, let us tell of the LORD's greatness; let us exalt his name together. PSALM 34:2-3

A prayer about MEDITATION
When I want to fix my thoughts on God

LORD GOD,

I don't want to just study about you. I want to be in communion with you! I know that is what ultimately leads me to godly actions. Help me to remember you first thing in the morning and to fall asleep with you still on my mind. May I meditate on you, my source of all hope. I want to think about you with a thankful heart whether I have plenty or little; I want to remember your great love for me. May I weave you into the fabric of my life so that my family will learn to love you with a grateful heart. As I meditate on you and your Word, keep my spiritual walk strong and focused. I long to be close to you.

I recall all you have done, O LORD; I remember your wonderful deeds of long ago. They are constantly in my thoughts. I cannot stop thinking about your mighty works.

PSALM 77:11-12

✓ A prayer about PURPOSE

When I want to discover what God has created me to do

HEAVENLY FATHER,

I am so busy—sometimes downright frenzied. At the end of another frantic day, I fall into bed and ask myself, *What did I do today? Did I make any difference?* My life often seems to lack a compelling purpose, a purpose worthy of my being created in your image. This aimlessness can lead me to apathy or even despair. This is not where I want to be, Lord. I believe that you have a purpose for my life. You have given me spiritual gifts, and you want me to use them to contribute to those around me. You call me to partner with you in your great redemptive plan for the world. What a privilege! May this call fuel my energy and ignite my dreams. As I use my gifts to help you fulfill this purpose, may I grow in my understanding of what is truly important for me to accomplish each day. Renew my work with a deeper sense of meaning so that I may labor for you wholeheartedly.

My dear brothers and sisters, be strong and immovable. Always work enthusiastically for the Lord, for you know that nothing you do for the Lord is ever useless.

I CORINTHIANS 15:58

A prayer about RESPECT
When I want godly respect

LORD GOD,
Having others respect me is not a bad thing, but when that becomes my ultimate goal, I'm going about my life the wrong way. So often you turn conventional worldly wisdom on its head. For example, your Word tells me that the last will be first and that leaders should not lord it over the ones they lead. Teach me, Lord, that I can't find respect by demanding it or grabbing for it. Instead, help me to understand that I will gain respect when I serve others rather than seeking to be served, or when I take responsibility for my actions rather than trying to save face in front of others. I will gain respect by speaking up when things are wrong instead of blending in with the group, or when I build others up instead of trying to make myself look good. Cause me to keep my eyes on you and not on myself, so that I will act in a way that brings me respect. But may I seek it for your glory, that others might see you working in me, and not for my own importance.

Those who are last now will be first then, and those who are first will be last. MATTHEW 20:16

A prayer about SPIRITUAL GIFTS
When I want to use my gifts for God

LORD,
I want to be available to you. I know one way I can do that is by developing the gifts you have given me so that I will be prepared for you to use me. Thank you that you give each believer at least one spiritual gift, and you also provide a place to use that gift to encourage others and to bring glory to your name. Give me wisdom as I seek to find the place I should serve. I know that when I use my gifts, I will help fulfill the purpose for which you made me. I'm thankful that I can never use up my spiritual gifts; rather, the more I use them, the more they grow.

A spiritual gift is given to each of us so we can help each other. To one person the Spirit gives the ability to give wise advice; to another the same Spirit gives a message of special knowledge. The same Spirit gives great faith to another, and to someone else the one Spirit gives the gift of healing. . . . In fact, some parts of the body that seem weakest and least important are actually the most necessary.
1 CORINTHIANS 12:7-9, 22

A prayer about GROWTH
When I want to grow spiritually

LORD,
Sometimes I get impatient with my spiritual growth because I can't see much change from one week to the next. But I know that, just like physical growth, spiritual growth starts small and grows a little at a time, day by day. I pray for the discernment to recognize the progress I have made and the patience to rest in the ongoing transformation. Remind me that I need nourishment to grow. Help me to challenge myself to study your Word, ask questions about it, and seek answers through prayer and the counsel of other believers. Teach me that each day is a building block; when I commit to building a life of godly character one day at a time, I will grow more and more spiritually mature. Thank you that the work is not all up to me. You are faithful to work in my heart, giving me the desire to please you. Spiritual growth is your goal for me, and you will bring it to fruition.

We ask God to give you complete knowledge of his will and to give you spiritual wisdom and understanding. Then the way you live will always honor and please the Lord, and your lives will produce every kind of good fruit. All the while, you will grow as you learn to know God better and better. COLOSSIANS 1:9-10

DAY 300 *Prayerful Moment*

✓ A prayer about WORRY

When worry overwhelms me

MERCIFUL GOD,

Worry is overwhelming me today. Most of the things I worry about never even happen, so I'm wasting my time and emotional energy for nothing. O Lord, when I feel consumed with worry, teach me to make a conscious effort to turn those thoughts into prayer. When I tell you my concerns, help me turn them over to you to handle. I know there is no problem that you cannot overcome. If you, almighty God, are taking care of me, I have no need to worry.

The LORD keeps watch over you as you come and go, both now and forever. PSALM 121:8

DAY 301 *Prayerful Moment*

✓ A prayer about LOVE

When I want to express my love for God

FATHER GOD,

How can I show you that I love you? Just as acts of service can show my family members that I love them, so obedience to your commands can express my love for you. But may I never confuse that with trying to *earn* your love by doing good works. You already love me, and nothing I do can change that! Because of your great love, I want to please you.

This is what [the Lord] requires of you: to do what is right, to love mercy, and to walk humbly with your God.
MICAH 6:8

✓ A prayer about DIGNITY
When I'm searching for dignity

LORD GOD,
When I feel as if I've lost my sense of dignity, it's usually because I've started basing my worth on others' opinions. I recognize in myself the human tendency to rank others from important to insignificant, but that kind of evaluation is not your way. You have created every human being on earth in your image, and that gives each of us immense worth and significance in your eyes. As I seek dignity, may I remember that it has two sides—first, accepting my own worth as you see me, and second, recognizing that same worthiness in others. May I see others as you do, worthy of my love and respect no matter where they live, what they look like, or what they do. When I behave respectably, have self-control and strong faith, and am loving and patient, then I'm showing dignity. May I realize anew that your esteem and approval are all I need.

God created human beings in his own image. In the image of God he created them; male and female he created them.
GENESIS 1:27

A prayer about COMPLACENCY

When I'm struggling to care about things that matter

FATHER GOD,

Apathy has set in, and I've lost my sense of passion and purpose. Apathy has drained me of motivation and excitement. I feel stuck, but I know you have the power to rescue me. I've believed Satan's lie that following you is nothing to be excited about. The truth is, following you is the *only* thing to be excited about! When I rehearse your wonderful work in my life—your salvation, your loving-kindness, your watchful care—my excitement is rekindled. I know that it is only through following you and serving you that my life will have meaning, energy, and purpose. Your Word describes the antidote to apathy: purposeful work, a thankful heart, and service to others. O Lord, please help me fight off feelings of apathy. Renew my focus on your purpose for my life, and cause me to anticipate with excitement the blessings you have in store for me.

God is not unjust. He will not forget how hard you have worked for him and how you have shown your love to him by caring for other believers, as you still do. Our great desire is that you will keep on loving others as long as life lasts, in order to make certain that what you hope for will come true. Then you will not become spiritually dull and indifferent.

HEBREWS 6:10-12

A prayer about HARD-HEARTEDNESS

When I want to guard against becoming hard-hearted

O LORD,

Is my heart becoming harder and more stubborn or softer and more pliable? Like the Prodigal Son's older brother, at times I find it hard to forgive others because my mind is set on punishment rather than mercy. Sometimes I struggle to see you in my daily life, choosing instead to interpret circumstances as coincidence or good luck. I'm afraid that means my heart is harder than it should be. I need your help, Lord! I want to have a tender heart that values mercy and forgiveness as you do, that reaches out to you no matter what my circumstances may be. Please keep me responsive to your love. May I never cut myself off from you, the only one who can really help me.

The older brother . . . replied, "All these years I've slaved for you and never once refused to do a single thing you told me to. And in all that time you never gave me even one young goat for a feast with my friends. Yet when this son of yours comes back after squandering your money on prostitutes, you celebrate by killing the fattened calf!" His father said to him, "Look, dear son, you have always stayed by me, and everything I have is yours. We had to celebrate this happy day. For your brother was dead and has come back to life! He was lost, but now he is found!" LUKE 15:28-32

DAY 305

A prayer about HURTS
When I need healing

MERCIFUL GOD,

You call me to practice the art of forgiveness. When someone has hurt me, your Word tells me that extending true forgiveness is the best way to melt away my hard feelings and experience the joy of restoration. I believe this truth, but it's so difficult to put into practice. I need you to soften my heart. Remind me that I have sinned against you and others and that, even though my sins have hurt you greatly, you have already offered me your complete forgiveness, and you desire to fully restore your relationship with me. If you have pardoned my great debt, how much more do I need to pardon those who sin against me? Lord, in this world I will experience pain. But when I am hurt by a friend, loved one, or even a stranger, it's a reminder that I long for a more perfect relationship with you, the one who will never hurt me or disappoint me.

Make allowance for each other's faults, and forgive anyone who offends you. Remember, the Lord forgave you, so you must forgive others. COLOSSIANS 3:13

A prayer about WORTH

When I'm trying to measure up

HEAVENLY FATHER,

It's hard for me to believe that your approval doesn't depend on what I do. I can get so caught up in the experience of serving you that I lose sight of the greatest privilege of all—knowing you and being known by you. May I never forget that having my name registered as a citizen of heaven means that I belong, without question, to your eternal Kingdom. Thank you, Lord! Nothing else I do on earth can compare with that privilege or joy. Free me from the trap of basing my identity and self-worth on my performance. I rejoice that my worth is based solely on your unconditional love.

There is no condemnation for those who belong to Christ Jesus. And because you belong to him, the power of the life-giving Spirit has freed you from the power of sin that leads to death. The law of Moses was unable to save us because of the weakness of our sinful nature. So God did what the law could not do. He sent his own Son in a body like the bodies we sinners have. And in that body God declared an end to sin's control over us by giving his Son as a sacrifice for our sins.

ROMANS 8:1-3

DAY 307 *Prayerful Moment*

✓ A prayer about RIGHT CHOICES

When I want to choose what is best

LORD,

I want to be a woman who looks beyond what is popular and who pursues what is godly. Teach me that what is best for me and those around me will always be consistent with what is right and good. Grant me the courage to stand up for what is right. Guard me from making choices based on what is easy; help me always to choose what is best.

Teach me how to live, O LORD. Lead me along the right path. PSALM 27:11

DAY 308 *Prayerful Moment*

✓ A prayer about INSPIRATION

When I consider how God inspires me

LORD,

I praise you for the diverse beauty in nature, which stirs me to worship you. I thank you for your Word because it contains instruction, guidance, and correction and inspires me to follow you. I'm grateful for the Holy Spirit, who dwells within me and encourages me with hope, comfort, wisdom, and love. You are my inspiration, helping me look beyond day-to-day details to the bigger picture of your love and majesty.

Those who live at the ends of the earth stand in awe of your wonders. From where the sun rises to where it sets, you inspire shouts of joy. PSALM 65:8

DAY 309

✓ ## A prayer about RISK
When I need to take risks for God

ALMIGHTY GOD,

I admit that most of the time I try to minimize risk. I have insurance policies, retirement funds, security codes on my credit cards, alarms in my home and car. These aren't bad things, but sometimes my desire to protect myself keeps me from doing what I should do. I feel hemmed in by my fear, and it prevents me from following what I know is your call. This is not where I want to be, Lord. Your Word says that following you is sometimes full of risk, but I know the risk is worth it if it helps me grow spiritually and be successful in your eyes. When you call me to do something that's outside my comfort zone, give me the courage to obey, even at the risk of failing. May I trust you to help me complete what you have asked me to do. I know that when I act in faith, you will reward me by causing my faith to grow.

Commit everything you do to the LORD. Trust him, and he will help you. PSALM 37:5

A prayer about SEEKING GOD
When I want to know God more

LORD GOD,

You are majestic and powerful, yet compassionate and gracious. Your thoughts are so far above mine that I will never be able to plumb the depths of your wisdom and love. I want to know you more. And your Word promises that when I seek you, I will find you. May I seek to discover you through your Word, which is filled with accounts of your actions throughout history, your concern for individuals, your plans for creation, your promises, and your commands. Teach me always to turn to the Bible when I want to know more of your character, your redemptive plan, and your truth. I will never know you fully in this life, but as I read your Word and spend time with you, my knowledge of you will grow—as will my desire to seek you.

My child, listen to what I say, and treasure my commands. Tune your ears to wisdom, and concentrate on understanding. Cry out for insight, and ask for understanding. Search for them as you would for silver; seek them like hidden treasures. Then you will understand what it means to fear the LORD, *and you will gain knowledge of God.*

PROVERBS 2:1-5

A prayer about ETERNITY

When I consider how my hope of eternity affects my present life

LORD GOD,

The hope of heaven changes everything. If this earthly life were all I had to live for, my every moment would be focused on the here and now, on temporary pleasure and material gain. But through your promises and Jesus' death on the cross, I have the free gift of eternal life. That puts all my troubles in perspective. My future is secure. No matter what happens in this life, I have peace. I am no longer controlled by my sinful nature, but I'm free to live as you want me to live. Thank you, Lord! May I be continually reminded of the hope of heaven and of eternal life in your presence, and may that transform my attitude toward my present circumstances.

God loved the world so much that he gave his one and only Son, so that everyone who believes in him will not perish but have eternal life. God sent his Son into the world not to judge the world, but to save the world through him.

JOHN 3:16-17

✓ A prayer about GUIDANCE

When I want to know the details of God's plan for my life

FATHER GOD,

I want to experience your guidance, and I know a big part of that is learning to trust you. That means trusting your directions, even when I can't see the destination. I don't know what you have in store for me, but maybe that's for the best. If I could see too much of my future, I might become afraid of the hard times ahead or overconfident about my accomplishments. I might be tempted to stop trusting your wisdom for my life. Instead of revealing everything, your guidance is like a flashlight that lights up just enough of the path ahead to show me where to take the next few steps. You reveal your plan in your own time, unfolding the joys and sorrows of life in doses I can handle. Lord, I can see from the circumstances around me that you have a plan for me and that you have my best interests in mind. I trust you to guide me every step of the way.

Your word is a lamp to guide my feet and a light for my path.
PSALM 119:105

A prayer about DEFEAT

When I feel as though I'm not experiencing success

HEAVENLY FATHER,

Often I find myself discontented because I want to be the best—the smartest, prettiest, best liked, fastest, most polished—and that simply isn't possible. Other times I'm discontented because I try to do something significant and end up failing. But I know it's neither realistic nor healthy to expect things to always go just as I'd like. The truth is, failing can help me stay humble and dependent on you. If I always succeeded, I might become arrogant and overly confident in myself. Keep me from that! I ask that you would use my times of defeat to grow my character. Teach me to be humbly dependent on you. Show me how to accept the woman I am, with the unique gifts and abilities you have given me. May I rely on you fully.

You ought to know, dear brothers and sisters, about the trouble we went through in the province of Asia. We were crushed and overwhelmed beyond our ability to endure, and we thought we would never live through it. In fact, we expected to die. But as a result, we stopped relying on ourselves and learned to rely only on God, who raises the dead. And he did rescue us from mortal danger, and he will rescue us again. We have placed our confidence in him, and he will continue to rescue us. 2 CORINTHIANS 1:8-10

DAY 314 *Prayerful Moment*

✓ A prayer about LISTENING
When I want to listen closely to God

LORD GOD,
I talk to you often, yet I'm not always good at listening for what you would like to say to me. But you are the only source of wisdom; I have so much to learn from you! Help me to find times to be quiet so that I will hear your voice. Give me the self-discipline to remove myself from distractions so that I can hear your gentle whisper in the quietness of my heart. Teach me, Lord, to wait expectantly for you. I know that the more I listen, the more I will hear.

Each morning I bring my requests to [the Lord] and wait expectantly. PSALM 5:3

✓ DAY 315 *Prayerful Moment*

A prayer about HELPLESSNESS
When I don't know what to do

LORD GOD,
I'm worn down by my circumstances, and I feel helpless. When I look at my situation, I am without hope and I'm blind to the many ways in which you may already be helping me. Give me insight to see my situation from your perspective, Lord. As I look through the eyes of faith, I know I will find the hope and help only you can give.

LORD, you know the hopes of the helpless. Surely you will hear their cries and comfort them. PSALM 10:17

DAY 316

A prayer about DESTINY
When I wonder what's in my future

FATHER GOD,
I hear the word *destiny* being used around me, usually meaning fate, or the purpose people are intended to fulfill. Your Word tells me that I have a destiny too—to share with you in all the wonders and comforts of your Kingdom forever. How amazing! Teach me to embrace this destiny and pursue it wholeheartedly. As I do, may I learn to set my priorities with eternity in view rather than on satisfying worldly desires. Purify my heart and my motives, and enable me to enjoy each day in your sustaining love. I'm thankful that I can live my life to the fullest with absolute confidence that death is not the end but only the beginning! No one can take me away from you. May this confidence give me meaning and hope as I persevere through the troubles of this life.

[Jesus said,] "My sheep listen to my voice; I know them, and they follow me. I give them eternal life, and they will never perish. No one can snatch them away from me, for my Father has given them to me, and he is more powerful than anyone else. No one can snatch them from the Father's hand."

JOHN 10:27-29

A prayer about AFFIRMATION
When I need affirmation

HEAVENLY FATHER,

You chose to create me in your image and to be in relationship with me. You have drawn me to yourself, even sacrificing your own Son to die for me. You have pursued me, rescued me from sin, and restored me! I am overflowing with thankfulness. When I am discouraged and need affirmation, remind me to read your words in the Bible and think about all you have done to show me how much I matter to you. When I realize how fully you value me, your love will break through the world's lies that try to tell me what I ought to be. Then, with your help, I will become the woman you created me to be.

See how very much our Father loves us, for he calls us his children, and that is what we are! . . . We know what real love is because Jesus gave up his life for us.
1 JOHN 3:1, 16

DAY 318

A prayer about DECEPTION

When I realize that I've been deceiving myself

LORD GOD,

When I think I can disobey you and not suffer the consequences, I'm deceiving myself. When I live as though this world is all there is, I'm deceiving myself. When I think I can ignore you and still receive all your blessings, I'm deceiving myself. O Lord, give me the wisdom to perceive when I'm falling prey to deception; open my eyes to see what is true. May materialism and the pursuit of pleasure never blind me to the realities of your wisdom, guidance, holiness, and justice. Allow me to open my heart to your Word, that your truth may break through the lies to help me see my life from your perspective. I praise you that your truth will always prevail.

Don't be misled—you cannot mock the justice of God. You will always harvest what you plant. Those who live only to satisfy their own sinful nature will harvest decay and death from that sinful nature. But those who live to please the Spirit will harvest everlasting life from the Spirit.

GALATIANS 6:7-8

DAY 319

✓ A prayer about ASSURANCE

When I need to be assured of God's unchanging love

LOVING GOD,

Your Word tells me that I can always be certain of your love for me. When I go through hard times, I sometimes feel as though you have abandoned me, but you have promised never to leave me so I trust you are near. Hard times reveal my need for your infinite love and care for me. In the midst of the pain and difficulty, teach me to pay attention so that I can see you working and feel your support. You have also provided some wonderful people in my life, and I'm thankful for the assurance I receive from them. I know, though, that you are the only one I can trust completely without fear of being disappointed. Your love gives me security for today and for eternity.

O Israel, the one who formed you says, "Do not be afraid, for I have ransomed you. I have called you by name; you are mine. When you go through deep waters, I will be with you. When you go through rivers of difficulty, you will not drown. When you walk through the fire of oppression, you will not be burned up; the flames will not consume you. For I am the LORD, your God, the Holy One of Israel, your Savior."

ISAIAH 43:1-3

✔ A prayer about ACCOUNTABILITY

When I consider my accountability to God

HEAVENLY FATHER,

I sometimes shy away from accepting accountability because it feels restrictive. It also forces me to open up dark corners of my life that I'd prefer to keep hidden, but I know that's the very reason accountability is so necessary. Giving an account of myself to a mature believer I can trust will help me make better decisions. Ultimately, Lord, I know accountability means answering to you. You know all the secrets of my heart anyway—why do I ever try to hide from you? Teach me to be honest with you and tell you about my struggles. Give me ears to listen to your voice as I read your Word and find guidance for living, guard me from doing something I will later regret, and guide me into the right path.

Search me, O God, and know my heart; test me and know my anxious thoughts. Point out anything in me that offends you, and lead me along the path of everlasting life.

PSALM 139:23-24

DAY 321 *Prayerful Moment*

A prayer about AVAILABILITY
When I want to be available to God

LORD GOD,
I want you to be able to use me. Help me to reorient my life so that no matter what I do, I do it as service to you. I am eager to go where you send me and do whatever you call me to do. When I follow you with a willing heart, I know you will bless me—not because of my ability, but because of my *avail*ability.

Be strong and courageous, and do the work. Don't be afraid or discouraged, for the LORD God, my God, is with you. He will not fail you or forsake you. 1 CHRONICLES 28:20

✓ ## DAY 322 *Prayerful Moment*

A prayer about GOD'S MAJESTY
When I recognize the awesomeness of God

MIGHTY GOD,
You are strong, but I don't fear you as I might fear other powerful things such as a severe storm or a huge wave crashing on the shore. Your power is captivating—the more I see your awesomeness at work in the world around me, the more I desire to experience your empowering Spirit. I praise you for your mighty power! You rule over everything.

Who is like you among the gods, O LORD—glorious in holiness, awesome in splendor, performing great wonders?
EXODUS 15:11

✓ ## A prayer about CONTENTMENT
When I long to be satisfied

FATHER,

Whenever I ask myself, *How much is enough?* the answer always seems to be, *Just a little bit more.* I depend on material things to make me happy, but the truth is that the more I crave, the less satisfied I am. Your Word tells me that the deepest contentment and joy I can ever experience will come not from pursuing success, pleasure, or material possessions but from pursuing intimacy with you. O God, I want to be satisfied! You are sufficient for me, and my security rests only in you. Your love and your provision are unfailing. What more could I need? As you provide for my needs in times of plenty and times of want, may I stop asking for more but become thankful and content.

I have learned how to be content with whatever I have. I know how to live on almost nothing or with everything. I have learned the secret of living in every situation, whether it is with a full stomach or empty, with plenty or little. For I can do everything through Christ, who gives me strength.
PHILIPPIANS 4:11-13

DAY 324

A prayer about MYSTERY

When I realize how much I don't know about God

ALMIGHTY GOD,

Your ways are higher than my ways, and your thoughts are deeper than my thoughts. There is so much about you that I don't understand; your ways are mysterious to me. But why am I surprised by this? You are all-powerful and all-knowing! If I could completely understand your nature, you would not be the God who inspires my awe. If I knew everything about you or your plans for my life, I wouldn't need faith. O Father, may I accept that you have shown me all I need to know to believe in you. There is much I can learn as I study your Word, and I'm thankful that following you is a lifelong adventure of discovery. Yet ultimately, even as I pursue learning, I must rest in faith. I entrust myself to you even when I don't understand. I have faith that one day, in heaven, all mysteries will be revealed.

"My thoughts are nothing like your thoughts," says the LORD. "And my ways are far beyond anything you could imagine."
ISAIAH 55:8

A prayer about DELIVERANCE
When I need to experience God's deliverance

LORD JESUS,
When I think about deliverance, I think about the things you did when you were on earth. You saved people from the spiritual oppression by demons, the physical oppression of disease, the intellectual oppression of false religion, and the injustice of abusive leadership. I need deliverance from my circumstances, too, but most of all I need the greatest kind of deliverance: deliverance from my sin. Because I believe in your sacrifice on the cross, I believe that you have delivered me from the penalty of my sin—eternal separation from you—and that you can also deliver me from the evil forces in this world that oppress me. I am overwhelmed by the scope of this salvation! My heart overflows with gratitude to you.

[Jesus said,] "The Spirit of the LORD is upon me, for he has anointed me to bring Good News to the poor. He has sent me to proclaim that captives will be released, that the blind will see, that the oppressed will be set free, and that the time of the LORD's favor has come." LUKE 4:18-19

A prayer about SACRIFICE

When I think about what God has sacrificed for me

ALMIGHTY GOD,

When I sacrifice something, I give it up to obtain something of greater value. I might be willing to hold off buying a new car to save money for my child's education, or to give up my time to help someone else. But I'm awed when I consider what you were willing to sacrifice for me. I don't always take sin as seriously as I should, but your Word tells me that sin brings eternal death because it separates people from you. In Old Testament days, you provided animal sacrifice as a way to remove their sins so they could be holy in your eyes. But when Jesus died on the cross, he transferred all my sins onto himself. His sacrifice was perfect; another will never be needed. I praise you, Lord, for sacrificing your Son to make atonement for my sin. I recognize my wrongdoing and accept your gift of forgiveness. And whenever I give up something for you or another person, may I be reminded of your great sacrifice for me.

Just as each person is destined to die once and after that comes judgment, so also Christ died once for all time as a sacrifice to take away the sins of many people. He will come again, not to deal with our sins, but to bring salvation to all who are eagerly waiting for him. HEBREWS 9:27-28

DAY 327

A prayer about PRAYER
When I wonder what prayer changes

LORD GOD,
When I've prayed for something for a long time and haven't seen the answer I'd hoped for, I'm tempted to wonder what good prayer really is. But I know that's a selfish way to look at it. There's so much more to prayer than just getting an answer to a question or a solution for a problem. The act of praying can change me. Thank you, God, that you can soften my heart through prayer and help me avoid the debilitating effects of anger, resentment, and bitterness. Help me to persevere in talking to you and in listening to you so that I may gain a greater understanding of myself, my situation, my motivation, your nature, and your direction for my life.

Don't worry about anything; instead, pray about everything. Tell God what you need, and thank him for all he has done. Then you will experience God's peace, which exceeds anything we can understand. His peace will guard your hearts and minds as you live in Christ Jesus. PHILIPPIANS 4:6-7

DAY 328 *Prayerful Moment*

✓ A prayer about MEANING

When I want my life to have more meaning

HEAVENLY FATHER,

My soul thirsts for meaning. I don't want to waste my life; rather, I want to live with purpose. You are the creator of all life, including my life, so only you can teach me how to live in a meaningful way. I ask you, Lord, to reveal your truth to me. Fulfill your purpose in me. Help me to grasp what is important to you. That's what I need to pursue; that's what will satisfy.

I cry out to God Most High, to God who will fulfill his purpose for me. PSALM 57:2

DAY 329 *Prayerful Moment*

✓ A prayer about GRATITUDE

When I want to cultivate a grateful heart

LORD,

When I take the time to appreciate the little things around me, I experience you in a new way. Turning my focus outward helps me see how many things I have to be thankful for. Help me, Lord, to cultivate a grateful heart, and help me to say "I'm thankful" more often, which will breed gratitude, rather than "I wish," which breeds discontent.

It is good to give thanks to the LORD, to sing praises to the Most High. It is good to proclaim your unfailing love in the morning, your faithfulness in the evening. PSALM 92:1-2

✓ A prayer about ADVERSITY
When I need God's strength to help me cope

HEAVENLY FATHER,
Sometimes in the midst of adversity, I cry out, "Where are you when I need you most?" But the answer is always the same: You are right beside me. You are there, giving me the power to help me cope. You don't promise to save me *from* trouble; instead, you tell me that you will be with me *when* I go through the deep waters that come my way. Lord, I know myself. If you acted like a genie in a bottle, granting my every wish, I would follow you for the wrong reasons and my character would never grow. You promise to be with me, which is so much better. Thank you for being with me in my troubles. Please give me wisdom to cope, strength to conquer my problems, and eyes of faith to see how I will become stronger as I walk with you and learn to deal with adversity.

In my distress I cried out to the LORD; yes, I prayed to my God for help. He heard me from his sanctuary; my cry to him reached his ears. PSALM 18:6

A prayer about RESPONSIBILITY
When I need to take ownership of my actions

FATHER GOD,

A lot of things influence me against taking responsibility for my own actions. It's easy for me to excuse my sins by saying, "Oh, it's just a bad habit." Sometimes I believe one of Satan's great lies: that I am a victim who has no power to resist my impulses. The world often teaches that my family, my environment, or my circumstances excuse me from responsibility. But your Word makes clear that what I do is a result of my choices and that I am responsible for those choices. Impress this on my heart, Lord, so that I may no longer make excuses for my actions but may face them head on. I am not powerless, for you are with me! You are more powerful than anything else that seeks to control me. May I tap into your power through prayer and be humble enough to ask for the support of fellow believers. When I do this, you will break the chains that hold me, and you will empower me to develop the strength to say no to temptations.

Don't you realize that you become the slave of whatever you choose to obey? You can be a slave to sin, which leads to death, or you can choose to obey God, which leads to righteous living. ROMANS 6:16

✓ A prayer about ADVICE

When I question whether I need advice from others

DEAR LORD,

I know I'm not wise enough to anticipate all the possibilities of a situation or grasp all the issues related to a problem. Yet sometimes I still question whether I need to listen to others. Father, just as you did for the people in Moses' day, you can use the advice of a trained counselor or a trusted friend as a turning point in my life. Right counsel that's consistent with your Word can make the difference between success and failure, joy and sorrow, prosperity and poverty, victory and defeat. So please prepare me for the wisdom I need to hear, from the person you have prepared to give it. May I be ready to receive it, and let it penetrate my heart.

[Moses' father-in-law said to Moses,] "This job is too heavy a burden for you to handle all by yourself. Now listen to me, and let me give you a word of advice, and may God be with you. . . . Select from all the people some capable, honest men who fear God and hate bribes. . . . They will help you carry the load, making the task easier for you. If you follow this advice, and if God commands you to do so, then you will be able to endure the pressures, and all these people will go home in peace." EXODUS 18:18-19, 21-23

A prayer about INVOLVEMENT

When I consider how I can be involved in God's Kingdom

DEAR LORD,

I'm amazed when I realize that you give every believer the opportunity to be involved in your Kingdom work. Your Word is clear about many things that are near to your heart and that I should care about as well: taking care of your creation, caring for the needy, defending and upholding justice, exercising my spiritual gifts for the good of the church, joining in worship and fellowship with other believers, and living as an example to those who do not know Christ. I want to care about the things that are important to you, Lord. It's easier to stand on the sidelines, but grant me the courage to get involved with things that are important to you. I want to reflect your priorities and your love to those around me. Teach me to be especially sensitive to a tug on my heart that means you are urging me to get involved in a specific task. May I have the privilege of helping others experience your comfort and hope and salvation.

Learn to do good. Seek justice. Help the oppressed. Defend the cause of orphans. Fight for the rights of widows.

ISAIAH 1:17

A prayer about SENSITIVITY

When I want to become more sensitive to others

HEAVENLY FATHER,

It's easy for me to be wrapped up in myself, but I want to become more sensitive to the needs of those around me. I know that involves being alert to people and responding appropriately to their feelings, but I need you to prompt me and show me how. May I learn to listen to others and consider the ways their situations are affected by their emotions and circumstances. May I show respect for people and their perspectives and be willing to lay aside my own needs to treat, with gentleness and care, those who are suffering. When I am compassionate, I am reflecting your character, so I know you will equip me in special ways to meet others' needs. As I put aside my own agenda, listen carefully, and act thoughtfully, please develop in me the kind of sensitive heart that touches others when they need it most.

All of you should be of one mind. Sympathize with each other. Love each other as brothers and sisters. Be tender-hearted, and keep a humble attitude. 1 PETER 3:8

DAY 335 *Prayerful Moment*

A prayer about ATTITUDE
When I need a better attitude

LORD GOD,

I know that how I view my problems determines my outlook on life. If I see them as obstacles, I will develop an attitude of bitterness, cynicism, and hopelessness. But if I see problems as a crucible for strengthening my character and my convictions, I will learn to rise above them. Even when it's hard to be thankful for the hard times, teach me how to be thankful *in* them because you are refining me.

Be thankful in all circumstances, for this is God's will for you who belong to Christ Jesus. 1 THESSALONIANS 5:18

DAY 336 *Prayerful Moment*

A prayer about MERCY
When I'm overwhelmed by God's mercy

LORD,

You are merciful beyond belief. You pour out your compassion on people—like me—who deserve your judgment. Instead of punishment, you extend forgiveness and the offer of eternal life. I praise you that your mercies never end! You never stop lavishing on me your faithful presence, provision for my needs, and hope for my future. You sustain my life. My very breath is a merciful gift from you!

The faithful love of the LORD never ends! His mercies never cease. Great is his faithfulness; his mercies begin afresh each morning. LAMENTATIONS 3:22-23

✓ A prayer about BALANCE
When I seek the blessings of a balanced life

FATHER,
Sometimes I get too focused on myself, and then I feel off balance. When I'm constantly thinking about what I can't have, shouldn't have, or will never have, I feel dissatisfied—and then my eyes are cemented even more firmly on myself. I know this causes me to neglect one of your greatest mandates: to help others who are in need. Show me how to balance meeting my own needs for food, shelter, and clothing with meeting the needs of those around me. Open my eyes to ways I can reach out to others. When I reach the right balance, may I experience contentment with what I have and satisfaction from caring for others.

True godliness with contentment is itself great wealth. After all, we brought nothing with us when we came into the world, and we can't take anything with us when we leave it. So if we have enough food and clothing, let us be content.
1 TIMOTHY 6:6-8

✓ A prayer about CONFIDENCE

When I need confidence to face life without fear

DEAR GOD,

I want to find the confidence that comes from you. Sometimes my prideful self-assurance leads to boasting, and then I find myself full of fears—especially of being found out and embarrassed in front of others. But when I have the right kind of confidence, I have an inner assurance. I feel valuable to you, and I have a sure conviction of who I am. That kind of confidence does not come from pride; it comes from security in Christ. Thank you, Lord, for the security that comes from knowing that you have called me to belong to you. You equip me to work in your Kingdom by giving me skills and talents to carry out your purpose. As I do what you have called me to do, I have joy and assurance. I don't have to be afraid. With you by my side, I can boldly set out to do your work, assured that I am within your will.

Blessed are those who trust in the LORD and have made the LORD their hope and confidence. JEREMIAH 17:7

A prayer about HOSPITALITY
When I wonder what I can share with others

HEAVENLY FATHER,

At times I am intimidated by the idea of hospitality. I would like to open my home to people, but I hold back because I don't have the groceries on hand to make a large meal or because my house isn't as clean as it should be. I get worried about what others will think, even though I know that's the wrong mind-set. Remind me, Lord, that the most important part of hospitality is sharing your love with others. I want to be generous with what I have and enjoy the people I'm with. Teach me to focus on making others feel welcome through my presence rather than through my presentation. May I warmly convey your love through my words and actions.

A woman named Martha welcomed [Jesus and the disciples] into her home. Her sister, Mary, sat at the Lord's feet, listening to what he taught. But Martha was distracted by the big dinner she was preparing. She came to Jesus and said, "Lord, doesn't it seem unfair to you that my sister just sits here while I do all the work? Tell her to come and help me." But the Lord said to her, "My dear Martha, you are worried and upset over all these details! There is only one thing worth being concerned about. Mary has discovered it, and it will not be taken away from her." LUKE 10:38-42

✓ A prayer about LOVE

When I wonder where romance is found in a life of faith

FATHER GOD,

It's such a wonderful feeling when others express their affection for me, enjoy my company, and are captivated by me. That makes me feel confident, interesting, and lovable. I tend to think of this in human terms, but the more I read your Word, the more I realize that you yourself are a romantic who longs for a close relationship with me. You desire my company and are interested in the smallest details of my day—you want nothing more than to walk with me through this life and for all eternity! You say that I am precious to you, and I'm filled with awe at this thought. As I realize my value in your eyes, teach me to find confidence in your love for me, strength to be faithful to you, and deep hunger to know more of you. Thank you for your amazing love that meets my deepest needs.

[The Lord said,] "I will win her back once again. I will lead her into the desert and speak tenderly to her there. . . . I will make you my wife forever, showing you righteousness and justice, unfailing love and compassion. I will be faithful to you and make you mine, and you will finally know me as the LORD." HOSEA 2:14, 19-20

A prayer about SURRENDER

When I need to surrender to God to find true victory

LORD GOD,

I'm fighting two battles in my spiritual life, and surrender plays a part in both of them. One fight is against sin. Without your help, I surrender to sin and its deadly consequences. Thank you for your Holy Spirit within me, who will give me the power to resist sin's control. I'm ashamed to admit that my second spiritual battle is sometimes fighting against you and your will for me. I know it's foolish, but I do it because I'm trying to hold on to the illusion that I have some control over my life. In this case, surrender is necessary and positive. I never want to give in to sin, Lord, but please soften my heart so that I will freely give in to you. Help me to realize how powerless I am to defeat sin on my own. I know that only when I give you control of my life will I find true victory.

My old self has been crucified with Christ. It is no longer I who live, but Christ lives in me. So I live in this earthly body by trusting in the Son of God, who loved me and gave himself for me. GALATIANS 2:20

DAY 342 *Prayerful Moment*

A prayer about PURPOSE
When I want to live more purposefully

FATHER GOD,
I thirst for more understanding about my life. I want to know why you made me and what you call believers to do. But you have not left me without resources. Your Word will tell me exactly what I need to know to have a purposeful life. May I have the wisdom to apply it, that I may live with renewed energy and direction.

Cry out for insight, and ask for understanding. Search for them as you would for silver; seek them like hidden treasures.
PROVERBS 2:3-4

DAY 343 *Prayerful Moment*

A prayer about STRENGTH
When I need strength for today

FATHER GOD,
I know I'm wasting a lot of energy focusing on the past. The more regrets and worries I drag around, the heavier the load I will carry today and the less energy I will have for tomorrow. Please help me, Lord. Release me from my fears and regrets, and free me to work enthusiastically toward the future you have prepared for me.

Forgetting the past and looking forward to what lies ahead, I press on to reach the end of the race and receive the heavenly prize for which God, through Christ Jesus, is calling us.
PHILIPPIANS 3:13-14

✓ A prayer about ADMIRATION
When I want to be a woman that people admire

FATHER,
I want to be respected, and sometimes I'm tempted to try to demand that respect, especially from my family. But I know that's not your way. What can make me a woman whom others admire? I know that the most admirable thing I can do is to reflect your love as I faithfully serve others. I can offer your gentle touch and demonstrate your love when I see them from your perspective and love them as you do. I long to be used by you in that way! Teach me that my desire for respect and admiration will be met when I see that others are experiencing you through me.

As a result of your ministry, [believers] will give glory to God. For your generosity to them . . . will prove that you are obedient to the Good News of Christ. And they will pray for you with deep affection because of the overflowing grace God has given to you. 2 CORINTHIANS 9:13-14

A prayer about COMMITMENT
When I want to be fully committed to God

FATHER,

I long to be fully committed to you—to belong to you completely, never turning aside from your way or looking back at my old life. I know that being committed requires more than just saying I believe in something, that it involves giving my whole self—body and soul, including my mind, will, and emotions—to you for your use. I'm deciding to do that now, Lord. Please help me to follow up that decision with an act of my will. And may I follow through with determination regardless of the difficulty. I know this may be costly, but I want to be fully yours and glorify you with my life. Your Word tells me that you promise great blessings if I am faithful in my commitment to you.

Give yourselves completely to God, for you were dead, but now you have new life. So use your whole body as an instrument to do what is right for the glory of God. ROMANS 6:13

A prayer about EMOTIONS

When my emotions are overwhelming me

FATHER,

My emotions are nothing to be ashamed of; they are a good gift from you. I'm grateful for the ability to grieve when I am hurting, to rejoice in exuberance when I have something to celebrate, to feel fear when I need to beware of a legitimate threat, and to be outraged at injustice and wrongdoing. These are good and right uses of my emotions. You know that sometimes, though, I allow them too much freedom. My feelings can tempt me to seek the pleasures of sin, or I lose control and lapse into behavior that hurts me and others. That's where I am right now, Lord. I need your help to regain self-control. As you conform me to your image, teach me to use my emotions to reflect your character. Then I'll be able to love others in healthy ways. Please help me to understand my feelings and direct them productively, not destructively. May I guard my heart so that it will not be overwhelmed by out-of-control emotions but will follow diligently after you.

The Holy Spirit produces this kind of fruit in our lives: love, joy, peace, patience, kindness, goodness, faithfulness, gentleness, and self-control. There is no law against these things!

GALATIANS 5:22-23

A prayer about WORSHIP
When I remember why I need to worship God

HOLY GOD,

You have created all human beings to worship—to revere, adore, pay homage to, and obey you. People worship many things, but your Word is clear that you alone are worthy of praise. You are the creator of all, the ruler of the universe, the wise, loving God who is far greater than I can even imagine. You call me to worship you as you really are, according to your true person and nature, with other believers and on my own. As I learn to worship at any time and in any place, may I experience your presence. Teach me, Lord, to praise you whenever I see your wisdom, power, direction, care, and love working in the world around me. Then worship will become a way of life that deepens my relationship with you.

Oh, how great are God's riches and wisdom and knowledge! How impossible it is for us to understand his decisions and his ways! For who can know the LORD's thoughts? Who knows enough to give him advice? And who has given him so much that he needs to pay it back? For everything comes from him and exists by his power and is intended for his glory. All glory to him forever! Amen. ROMANS 11:33-36

A prayer about PATIENCE
When I'm feeling impatient

HEAVENLY FATHER,

So many things in my life make me impatient. Sometimes I get stuck in a traffic jam or have some other unexpected delay. Sometimes I have to wait for a child to mature past a troubled stage, or I have to deal with some other difficult situation that hangs on far longer than I think it should. I want all my problems to be resolved! I recognize these situations as obstacles that frustrate me, but if I have the right perspective, Lord, I can see them as opportunities to grow in patience. Please give me the grace to know when there's nothing I can do to speed up a situation and the patience to wait for your timing. I trust in the eternal plans you have for me. May the knowledge that my long-range future is settled and secure allow me to be more patient during today's frustrations.

We also pray that you will be strengthened with all his glorious power so you will have all the endurance and patience you need. May you be filled with joy, always thanking the Father. COLOSSIANS 1:11-12

DAY 349 *Prayerful Moment*

✓ A prayer about CHURCH
When I want to help my church

HEAVENLY FATHER,
You have given every believer special gifts. Some people are great organizers; others are gifted musicians, teachers, or even dishwashers. Teach me how important it is to use my gifts in my congregation. As we serve, may the church become a powerful force for good, a strong witness for you, and a mighty army to combat Satan's attacks. I am thankful that the body of Christ has a place for me.

Just as our bodies have many parts and each part has a special function, so it is with Christ's body. ROMANS 12:4-5

✓ DAY 350 *Prayerful Moment*

A prayer about PANIC
When I'm frightened

LORD GOD,
I'm experiencing panic, and I'm physically and emotionally paralyzed. I don't know how to deal with this fear, but I know you are with me. Your job is to rescue me; my job is just to trust you and then give you the credit for your help. What a comfort to know that I don't have to solve everything! As I rest in the knowledge that you are in control, I know I will experience peace instead of panic.

The LORD your God is living among you. He is a mighty savior. . . . With his love, he will calm all your fears.
ZEPHANIAH 3:17

A prayer about DIFFERENCES

When I'm in conflict with another person

FATHER,

You know I'm struggling in my relationships with a few people right now. Their point of view and approach to life are so different from mine that we clash, and I fear we may never be compatible. I'm frustrated by my inability to live in peace with them, and I need your help to respond to them with grace and patience. I take hope in the fact that you will one day restore camaraderie among even the greatest of enemies in the animal kingdom. If you have such a wonderful plan for the animals, how much more will you restore human relationships! I look forward in faith and hope to the day when all creation will live together in harmony. In the meantime, even as I struggle with these people, please empower me to treat them with love and to keep my words and actions above reproach.

The wolf and the lamb will feed together. The lion will eat hay like a cow. . . . In those days no one will be hurt or destroyed on my holy mountain. I, the LORD, have spoken!

ISAIAH 65:25

✓ A prayer about the HOLY SPIRIT
When I'm struggling to pray

HEAVENLY FATHER,

I am so upset, confused, and overwhelmed that I don't even know what to say to you. But I take great comfort in the fact that you hear, understand, and respond to my prayers, even when they're not polished or articulate. You see my heart, and you know me to the core. When I don't know what to ask for or even how to communicate my great need, I rest in the assurance from your Word that your Holy Spirit helps me pray. At times like these I lean on him—he understands my deepest longings and expresses them to you on my behalf. Thank you, God, for this remarkable reassurance that even in my deepest grief or greatest confusion, I am heard and understood.

The Holy Spirit helps us in our weakness. For example, we don't know what God wants us to pray for. But the Holy Spirit prays for us with groanings that cannot be expressed in words. And the Father who knows all hearts knows what the Spirit is saying, for the Spirit pleads for us believers in harmony with God's own will. ROMANS 8:26-27

DAY 353

✓ ## A prayer about VALUES
When I consider the power of godly values

LORD GOD,

What I say I value isn't always reflected in how I spend my time and money, who my friends are, or what I watch and read. I want my choices to reflect what I really consider important, useful, and worthwhile. Please give me the wisdom to see where the world's values have shaped me, and give me the courage and determination to change. You are my top priority, and I want that to be reflected in the words I speak and the things I do. O Lord, may others be able to look at how I spend my time, energy, and money and know that I love you. When I love and worship you, obey you wholeheartedly, make godly choices, and serve others, I display godly values. As I treasure you above all, may you use my life in a powerful way.

Store your treasures in heaven, where moths and rust cannot destroy, and thieves do not break in and steal. Wherever your treasure is, there the desires of your heart will also be.

MATTHEW 6:20-21

A prayer about REST
When I need rest

LOVING GOD,
So often I fall into the trap of living in a state of frenzied activity. I take pride in telling others how busy I am, and I feel guilty if I relax. But this isn't the way you created me to live! You set the example when you rested after creating the world. Your Word makes clear that you want me to take time for rest and refreshment for my body and soul. In Genesis you call rest "holy." Teach me, Lord, to rest—to stop working so that I may care for my physical and spiritual needs. I spend so much time taking care of others, but I need to pay attention to the health of my own soul too. If I neglect this, I will miss hearing your still, small voice and seeing you work in my heart. My life will become all busyness, and I'll miss out on the deeper meaning and purpose my life should have. I so deeply desire the refreshment you provide. Please give me the self-discipline to carve out regular times for worship and spiritual refreshment.

The LORD is my shepherd; I have all that I need. He lets me rest in green meadows; he leads me beside peaceful streams. He renews my strength. He guides me along right paths, bringing honor to his name. PSALM 23:1-3

DAY 355

A prayer about PERSPECTIVE

When I've become self-focused

HEAVENLY FATHER,

Sometimes I lose sight of you, and then my perspective on life doesn't line up with what's important and what's not, and I start to think that everything revolves around me. That kind of self-focus leads me to frustration, selfishness, and dissatisfaction. Help me to remember that obeying you is the only way to keep an accurate perspective on life. Teach me that obedience keeps me focused on what is really important, leads me to your will, and gives me an eternal orientation that affects the way I live here on earth. I know that all I really need is what you supply in great abundance. Please give me perspective on my days and a greater desire to obey you as I see the rewards of obedience.

[Jesus said,] "If you try to hang on to your life, you will lose it. But if you give up your life for my sake, you will save it."

MATTHEW 16:25

DAY 356 *Prayerful Moment*

✓ A prayer about ABILITIES
When I want to make the most of my abilities

LORD,
I know you are more concerned with my faith than with my abilities. You will use my abilities only in proportion to my faith in you. I want to delight you, and I know the way to do that is to say yes to you, to walk in faith, and then to watch you accomplish your will through me.

All glory to God, who is able, through his mighty power at work within us, to accomplish infinitely more than we might ask or think. EPHESIANS 3:20

DAY 357 *Prayerful Moment*

✓ A prayer about PLEASURE
When I'm enjoying the things God has given me

LOVING GOD,
This world is full of good things you have created for people to enjoy: countless beautiful scenes in nature, laughter, loving relationships, joy from watching a child grow, good food, and friends to share with, to name just a few. My heart is filled with gratitude, Lord. As I enjoy these blessings, I'm accepting your gifts to me—and I think you are pleased.

Since everything God created is good, we should not reject any of it but receive it with thanks. For we know it is made acceptable by the word of God and prayer.
1 TIMOTHY 4:4-5

A prayer about AFFIRMATION

When I want to affirm others

FATHER GOD,

I still remember encouraging words people have said to me at specific moments in my life. Those affirmations have refreshed me, energized me, and sometimes helped me see more clearly where or what you want me to be. I want to offer words of affirmation to others, too. As I notice and comment on others' strengths or spiritual growth, may my words come from a pure and tender heart, creating divine moments of encouragement for them. As I notice and affirm your work in believers' lives, I'll be led to praise you too!

[Paul said,] "I always thank my God when I pray for you, Philemon, because I keep hearing about your faith in the Lord Jesus and your love for all of God's people. And I am praying that you will put into action the generosity that comes from your faith as you understand and experience all the good things we have in Christ. Your love has given me much joy and comfort, my brother, for your kindness has often refreshed the hearts of God's people."

PHILEMON 1:4-7

A prayer about HOPE
When I need hope in the midst of trouble

O LORD JESUS,
I'm reassured to know that my troubles do not surprise you. After all, you said in John 16:33 that they are a fact of life in this fallen world. Instead of my focusing on problems, help me to look to you, the one who experienced some of the same troubles I do. If I am listening, you will show me how to have peace in spite of my situations. Even more than that, you will use these struggles to teach me endurance and to strengthen my character, making me more like you. I don't want these difficulties to be wasted, Lord. The Bible assures me that you will either deliver me from my troubles or bring me through them—for your glory and my joy. And that gives me hope!

We can rejoice, too, when we run into problems and trials, for we know that they help us develop endurance. And endurance develops strength of character, and character strengthens our confident hope of salvation. And this hope will not lead to disappointment. For we know how dearly God loves us, because he has given us the Holy Spirit to fill our hearts with his love. ROMANS 5:3-5

A prayer about PEACE

When I need relief during life's storms

LORD GOD,

So many things invade my life and affect my sense of peace—conflict, uncertainty, busyness, worry, and fear, to name just a few. Today I feel overcome with anxiety and stress. I'm sinking, Lord! How can I possibly have peace when I'm experiencing all this? Help me to fix my mind on Jesus' promise to his disciples: that he was leaving them with peace of mind and heart. That promise is for me, too, and I cling to it today as if it's a lifeline. I can't prevent difficulties from invading my life, but you remind me that I don't have to worry about the ultimate outcome. I know that you are in charge; the future is certain. May that give me a quiet, unshakable confidence. May the assurance of your love and your plan keep me from panicking, even in the midst of today's storms.

[Jesus said,] "I am leaving you with a gift—peace of mind and heart. And the peace I give is a gift the world cannot give. So don't be troubled or afraid. Remember what I told you: I am going away, but I will come back to you again."

JOHN 14:27-28

A prayer about COMFORT

When I consider how God comforts me

LORD GOD,

When I am brokenhearted and in need of comfort, you don't always act the way I might expect. Sometimes I anticipate that you'll comfort me by providing things I want or by changing my circumstances, but instead, your comfort often comes through your presence. And what better way is there? After all, circumstances are temporary, but you are eternal. My needs and wants are constantly changing, but you never change. Material things can provide comfort for a time, but you are the only source of comfort at *all* times. Whenever I need comfort, Lord, I'm awed that you show up—not with presents, but with your abiding presence.

Let all who fear the LORD repeat: "His faithful love endures forever." In my distress I prayed to the LORD, and the LORD answered me and set me free. The LORD is for me, so I will have no fear. What can mere people do to me? Yes, the LORD is for me; he will help me. PSALM 118:4-7

A prayer about CHALLENGES
When I consider how challenges shape my life

FATHER GOD,

I'm facing a difficulty right now, and I want to have the right attitude. May I see this situation not as a negative but as a tool you can use to hone me. Just as it takes the rough surface of a file to sharpen the blade of a knife, so it takes rough times to sharpen me into the kind of person you can use effectively. May each trouble bring me greater wisdom, more maturity to withstand the trials that come my way, and deeper trust in you. I know that as I endure troubles I will gain more and more courage to face whatever comes. May I always be willing to follow your leading into uncharted waters so that I can accomplish something unique and purposeful for you. Impress on my heart that the greatest challenges can become the greatest opportunities.

These trials will show that your faith is genuine. It is being tested as fire tests and purifies gold—though your faith is far more precious than mere gold. So when your faith remains strong through many trials, it will bring you much praise and glory and honor on the day when Jesus Christ is revealed to the whole world. 1 PETER 1:7

DAY 363 *Prayerful Moment*

A prayer about the FUTURE
When I need to trust God with my future

GOD,
You direct my steps. Although the path may lead me through dark valleys or appear to take unnecessary detours, I believe that one day I will look back and discover that your way was perfect. I put my future in your hands.

The LORD *says, "I will guide you along the best pathway for your life. I will advise you and watch over you."*
PSALM 32:8

DAY 364 *Prayerful Moment*

A prayer about FINISHING
When I want to finish well

LORD,
I know that life involves aging. That means facing the pain of realizing that I no longer possess the physical skills or the energy I used to have. As I near the final chapter of my life, Lord, may I look back and see your faithfulness. I pray for the grace to be a powerful witness to your mercy, your presence, and your constancy. Prepare me to finish well, with words of praise on my lips.

My life is an example to many, because you have been my strength and protection. PSALM 71:7

A prayer about DETERMINATION

When I am resolved to be victorious over Satan

LORD,

I want to be victorious over my struggles and temptations. Your Word makes clear that Satan is determined to gain and keep a foothold in my life, so I have to be even more resolved to drive him away. I'm confident that you are mightier than Satan; you will always defeat him. So I call on you, asking you to fill me with the power of your Holy Spirit. May I grow in my knowledge of Scripture and claim your promises of victory over sin. I need your strength and the armor you have provided, Lord, to fight the spiritual battles I face. The Bible tells me that you promise ultimate victory to all who believe in you and obey you. Please give me the courage and confidence to persevere to the end.

Be strong in the Lord and in his mighty power. Put on all of God's armor so that you will be able to stand firm against all strategies of the devil. For we are not fighting against flesh-and-blood enemies, but against evil rulers and authorities of the unseen world, against mighty powers in this dark world, and against evil spirits in the heavenly places.

EPHESIANS 6:10-12

TOPICAL INDEX

Abilities | Days 196, 356
Absolutes | Day 247
Acceptance | Days 135, 173
Accomplishments | Day 205
Accountability | Day 320
Adaptability | Day 15
Admiration | Day 344
Adoption | Day 276
Adversity | Day 330
Advice | Day 332
Affirmation | Days 317, 358
Amazement | Day 185
Ambition | Day 269
Anger | Day 115
Apology | Day 250
Appreciation | Day 146
Approval | Days 190, 216
Assurance | Days 188, 319
Attitude | Days 149, 335
Availability | Day 321
Balance | Day 337
Beauty | Day 267
Belonging | Day 191
Bible | Day 95
Blessings | Days 1, 218
Boredom | Day 144
Brokenness | Day 214
Burnout | Day 80
Busyness | Day 62
Caring | Day 168
Celebration | Day 147
Challenges | Days 3, 165, 362
Change | Day 223
Character | Days 14, 150
Children | Day 8
Choices | Days 73, 241, 307
Church | Days 70, 280, 349
Circumstances | Days 179, 209
Comfort | Days 151, 361
Commitment | Days 46, 152, 345
Communication | Day 43
Community | Day 22
Comparisons | Day 141
Compassion | Days 58, 195
Competition | Day 249
Complacency | Days 35, 161, 303
Compromise | Day 263
Confession | Day 11
Confidence | Days 56, 338
Conformity | Day 288
Confusion | Day 163
Conscience | Day 282
Contentment | Days 79, 323
Convictions | Day 210
Courage | Days 142, 292
Creativity | Day 203
Crisis | Days 60, 198
Criticism | Days 184, 204
Culture | Day 31
Deception | Day 318
Decisions | Day 221
Defeat | Day 313
Deliverance | Day 325
Denial | Day 239
Dependence | Day 266
Depression | Day 256
Desires | Day 192
Destiny | Day 316
Determination | Day 365
Differences | Days 17, 351
Dignity | Day 302
Disappointment | Day 240
Discernment | Day 217
Discipline | Days 59, 186
Discouragement | Days 53, 273
Distractions | Day 158
Diversity | Day 133
Doubt | Days 29, 215, 291
Emotions | Days 23, 346
Empathy | Day 283
Emptiness | Day 225
Encouragement | Days 63, 224

Endurance | Day 293
Enemies | Day 137
Enthusiasm | Day 160
Eternity | Days 50, 311
Evil | Day 145
Example | Day 259
Excellence | Days 166, 262
Experiencing God | Day 90
Failure | Day 260
Faith | Days 159, 265
Faithfulness | Days 84, 279, 287
Family | Day 244
Fasting | Day 110
Fatigue | Day 38
Fearing God | Day 226
Finishing | Days 268, 364
Flexibility | Day 124
Following God | Day 140
Forgiveness | Days 97, 113
Freedom | Days 55, 272
Friendship | Days 7, 36
Fun | Day 130
Future | Days 132, 363
Generosity | Day 229
Gentleness | Day 189
Goals | Day 2
God's Call | Days 139, 170
God's Care | Day 270
God's Forgiveness | Day 131
God's Hand | Days 75, 106, 278
God's Majesty | Day 322
God's Presence | Days 199, 231
God's Promises | Days 83, 172
God's Timing | Day 155
Goodness | Day 154
Gossip | Day 71
Grace | Day 24
Gratitude | Days 49, 252, 329
Growth | Day 299
Guidance | Day 312
Guilt | Day 197
Habits | Days 136, 228
Happiness | Day 290
Hard-Heartedness | Day 304
Healing | Day 4
Health | Day 44
Heart | Days 27, 125, 222
Heaven | Days 10, 20, 183
Help | Days 101, 230
Helplessness | Days 6, 315
Holiness | Day 169
Holy Spirit | Days 85, 352
Honesty | Day 40
Hope | Days 48, 359
Hospitality | Days 25, 339
Humility | Day 45
Hurts | Days 86, 305
Influence | Day 76
Initiative | Day 98
Inspiration | Days 255, 308
Integrity | Day 176
Intercession | Day 123
Intimacy | Day 274
Invitation | Day 113
Involvement | Days 164, 333
Joy | Days 119, 232
Judging Others | Day 109
Kindness | Days 128, 284
Letting Go | Day 234
Life's Demands | Day 13
Limitations | Day 87
Listening | Days 93, 171, 314
Loneliness | Days 18, 261
Loss | Day 68
Love | Days 100, 243, 301, 340
Loyalty | Day 47
Meaning | Day 328
Meditation | Days 174, 295
Memories | Day 126
Mentoring | Day 102
Mercy | Days 235, 336
Miracles | Days 257, 294
Mistakes | Day 206
Motivation | Days 129, 286
Motives | Day 213
Music | Day 69
Mystery | Day 324
Needs | Days 5, 91

Neglect | Day 138
Neighbors | Day 207
Obedience | Days 118, 238
Obstacles | Day 153
Opportunities | Day 64
Overwhelmed | Days 16, 67
Pain | Day 194
Panic | Day 350
Passion | Days 12, 281
Past | Days 156, 227
Patience | Days 233, 251, 348
Peace | Days 41, 104, 360
Perfection | Day 34
Persecution | Day 94
Perseverance | Day 201
Perspective | Days 99, 355
Plans | Day 54
Pleasure | Days 66, 357
Potential | Day 78
Power of God | Day 148
Praise | Days 28, 236
Prayer | Days 19, 289, 327
Priorities | Day 72
Purpose | Days 296, 342
Quietness | Days 26, 182
Quitting | Day 30
Reconciliation | Day 51
Regrets | Day 120
Relevance | Day 88
Renewal | Days 9, 108
Repentance | Day 111
Respect | Days 89, 297
Responsibility | Day 331
Rest | Days 127, 354
Rewards | Day 114
Risk | Day 309
Role Models | Day 181
Sacrifice | Day 326
Salvation | Day 220
Sanctification | Day 254
Satisfaction | Day 178
Security | Days 275, 285
Seeking God | Days 112, 310
Self-Esteem | Days 32, 193
Self-Sacrifice | Day 116
Sensitivity | Days 200, 334
Service | Days 42, 74, 92
Sharing | Day 121
Significance | Day 162
Simplicity | Day 208
Sorrow | Days 211, 246
Spiritual Disciplines | Day 219
Spiritual Gifts | Day 298
Spiritual Growth | Days 237, 248
Spiritual Warfare | Day 122
Strength | Days 271, 343
Strengths and Weaknesses | Day 61
Stubbornness | Day 96
Success | Day 37
Suffering | Day 157
Surprise | Day 177
Surrender | Days 33, 341
Temptation | Day 82
Tenderness | Day 180
Testing | Days 117, 202
Thoughts | Day 277
Time | Day 264
Tithing | Days 81, 143
Transformation | Day 245
Unity | Days 77, 242
Values | Day 353
Victory | Day 134
Vulnerability | Day 187
Will of God | Days 39, 253
Wisdom | Day 65
Witnessing | Day 212
Women | Day 105
Words | Day 175
Work | Days 57, 103, 258
Worry | Days 167, 300
Worship | Days 21, 107, 347
Worth | Days 52, 306